THE TRANSFORMING POWER OF LANGUAGE:
THE POETRY OF ADRIENNE RICH

The Transforming Power of Language:
The Poetry of Adrienne Rich

Myriam Díaz-Diocaretz

H&S
HES PUBLISHERS/UTRECHT
1984

ISBN 90 6194 394 9
© HES Publishers B.V. P.O. Box 129 3500 AC Utrecht/Netherlands

FOREWORD

The three essays that have been collected here are part of a larger project involving the analysis of feminist poetic discourse produced by North-American women writers. I hope they communicate to the reader the strength and innovative aspects of the poetry of Adrienne Rich in the past three decades. It may be useful to prescribe the limits I intend to place in these pages: they were born from different purposes but with the same intention in mind. They were provided, partly, by my experience of translating her poetry since 1975. They attempt to answer some questions on the nature and boundaries of feminist writing, its links with tradition, its originality; above all they deal with my notion of de-territorialization and re-territorialization in language, proposing the study of the displacement of connotations with reference to patriarchy as one of the major factors in the aesthetic spectrum of feminist discourse.

Adrienne Rich, one of the leading North-American poets, seems to me to embody the precise model to probe those given assumptions because her voice has generated artistic texts that range from non-feminist to female oriented.

The first essay, "From Verbal Art to Feminist Discourse" offers the reader a chronological view of Rich's main themes, her shifts, and further developments; without pretending to be exhaustive, I consider her twelve volumes of poetry up to the present, to guide the reader towards the general context of her work. The poet's concept of "revision" and the modes of existence of her texts are linked with the making of feminist ideology and some specific textual strategies.

The second, "The Poet and the Alien Text" is centered on the intertextual component of polemic and congenial dialogue, defining thus Rich's discourse in terms of her own readings and of her use of the intertextual factor for women's literary texts.

Finally, "No One's Fated or Doomed to Love Anyone" is a close reading of the Twenty-One Love Poems in which the speaker - as poet, and a dreamer - explores love as a dialectic of togetherness and separateness in a process of correlations of the unconscious, reality, and poetry.

While these essays are united by a recurrent objective to study women's literary discourse, my major concern remains the poetry of Adrienne Rich.

Myriam Díaz-Diocaretz
Amsterdam

INDEX

I.	From Verbal Art to Feminist Discourse	1
	Introduction	2
	1. Author-Function Spectrum	3
	2. Reading and Writing as Re-Vision and Program	17
	3. The Making of an Ideology	22
II.	The Poet and the Alien Text	31
	1. Intertextuality in Feminist Poetic Discourse	32
	2. The Intertextual Factor in the Poetry of Adrienne Rich	39
III.	"'No One's Fated or Doomed to Love Any Anyone': A Reading of 'Twenty-One Love Poems'"	51
	1. "The Meaning of Our Love"	52
	2. Limitless Desire, Limitless Language	56
Notes		65
References		69

I. FROM VERBAL ART TO FEMINIST DISCOURSE

INTRODUCTION

The development of Adrienne Rich's poetry can be seen in the light of a movement from artistic detachment to a radical lesbian/feminist position. Underlying this gradual change is the poet's notion of writing and literature as political acts both for writers and readers alike, as a necessary task to re-form a positive and integrated condition for women so that they can exist unrepressed and no longer silenced. Rich's stylistic and thematic developments are a reflection of the evolution of her ideas in relation to language and society:

> The necessity of poetry has to be stated òver and over, but only to those who have reason to fear its power, or those who still believe that language is "only words" and that an old language is good enough for our descriptions of the world we are trying to transform.
> (Rich 1979g:247)

To begin with, Adrienne Rich can be justly considered among the founders of contemporary discourse of feminist writing in the United States. In this, she follows the argumentative nature of creative texts as produced, for example, by George Eliot, Mary Wollstonecraft, Emily Dickinson, Virginia Woolf, writers who gave her a "kind of galvanizing force" (Bulkin 1977b:54). Particularly since the 1970's Rich chooses to identify mainly with women, and to write about women as subject and object of her discourse; yet it is important to notice that in the first two decades of her career as a writer, perhaps most strikingly during the 1950's, her poetry shows her greater concern for the expressive value of texts, assigning a minimal importance to having a particular kind of addressee. While criticism on her work has focused either on the imagistic and stylistic transformations, or on her themes, it will be quite instructive to follow Michel Foucault's suggestion of "reversing the traditional idea of the author" (Foucault 1979:159). A study of rich's discourse according to its modes of existence to where it has been used, and how it circulates will give us a *spectrum* of the activity of author-function (a term we borrow from Foucault, p. 158). That is, we can study the modes of functioning of

Rich's discourse and its system of dependencies by tracking the modes of circulation and the critical evaluation of her work, as well as the reader's appropriations of her discourse for themselves. Here we will attempt merely to outline the main areas in Adrienne Rich's author-function activity.

I.1. AUTHOR-FUNCTION SPECTRUM

In reference to the modes of circulation of Adrienne Rich's work, they begin to emerge in 1951 with her book A Change of World which was selected by W.H. Auden as winner of the Yale Younger Poets Award, and published by Yale University Press with a preface by Auden himself (Auden 1951). In 1955 she published The Diamond Cutters and Other Poems, for which she was awarded the Ridgely Torrence Memorial Award of the Poetry Society of America. Subsequently she received other important awards for her poetry (see Gelpi, 1975:203-204). In the years that follow, Rich produced several other volumes: Snapshots of a Daughter-in-Law (1963), Necessities of Life (1966), Selected Poems (1967), Leaflets (1969), The Will to Change (1971). Two years later, Rich published Diving into the Wreck (1973), for which she was given the 1974 National Book Award. On that occasion she "rejected the award as an individual, but accepted it, in a statement written with Audre Lorde and Alice Walker, two other nominees, in the name of all women". (Gelpi, 1975:204).

Adrienne Rich has become a well established poet whose books have been published in important editorial houses. Her poetry now circulates not only in book form, but has appeared in the most important poetry and literary journals of the United States.[1] After Diving into the Wreck, the poet began to publish primarily in feminist literary magazines.[2] A number of her poems and essays have appeared, since that period, first in chapbooks issued by small presses run by women (Rich 1976b, 1977a, 1977b). The poet is also a notable speaker (Gelpi, 1975:ix); her lectures and poetry readings from coast to coast in the United States, Europe, and Japan have attracted thousands of women in the last decade. Rich's poetry has broadly circulated also because she has been widely anthologized and translated, especially since the 1970's. Critical commentaries on her work abound, both in well-known American periodicals with large circulation and in feminist journals.

A Change of World

It is helpful to consider the critical evaluation of her work throughout the years, since this is part of the activity of the author-function. Her first book, A Change of World (1951) reflects what W.H. Auden celebrated as a "capacity for detachment from the self and its emotions without which no art is possible". (Auden, 1975:126). This detachment may be found in all those poems in her first volume, particularly "Storm Warnings", "Boundary", "Why Else But to Forestall This Hour", "The Rain of Blood". A Change of World contains different textual expressions of aesthetic distance; in the poem "At a Bach Concert" Rich concludes; "A too-compassionate art is half an art/Only such proud restraining purity/Restores the else-betrayed, too-human heart" (1975:7). Such is the world of the poet's voice in that period, a voice framed in the persona of an objective seer, one without gender-consciousness. The poem "Afterward" closes with the lines; "We who know limits now give room/To one who grows to fit his doom" (1975:5). Strikingly, this poem is changed when included in the 1975 edition, from the "he" to "she". Thus the last line reads "To one who grows to fit her doom". On this, Rich noted: "I have altered the pronouns not simply as a matter of fact but because they alter, for me, the dimensions of the poem" (1975:247). The same type of transformation was applied to "The Tourist and The Town", in The Diamond Cutters.

Often quoted in the critical research on Rich's detachment and technical mastery is "Storm Warnings", written in iambic pentameter lines:

>   Weather abroad
> And weather in the heart alike come on
> Regardless of prediction.
>
> Between foreseeing and averting change
> Lies all the mastery of elements

> Which clocks and weatherglass cannot alter.
> (1975:3)

This detachment, however, changes with the years, bringing about some significant changes in the subject and themes of her books. As the poet comments on her own work, she feels that her early poems are marked profoundly by objective and observant tone and craft (Rich, 1964, 1979b); she then finds that those poems were "queerly limited" because she had "surpressed, omitted, falsified even, certain disturbing elements, to gain the perfection of order" (in Gelpi, 1975:89). That perception of order was sought and shaped by rhetorical, sylistic and objectified thematic elements tacitly imposed by the established poetic tradition and that were passively accepted by the poet. W.H. Auden's praise of Rich's use of craft represents the common ground of the critical reception of her first three books (Cf. Jarrell, 1965; Gelpi, 1973; Boyers, 1973; Vendler, 1973). Rich (1979b:40) later explains that "formalism ... was part of the strategy", of distancing herself from her subject matter. Becoming concious of self-censorship impelled her to find the language and the images that would allow her to express her awareness of the "oppressive nature of the male/female relations" (Rich, 1979b:35). Thus she grows more and more involved in the search for what she feels is a more accurate vision of the self she discovers in relation to the patriarchal world.

The Diamond Cutters

In The Diamond Cutters (1955), her second book, the poet still uses formal strategies (use of *personae*, objective perspective) to distance her emotions, as in A Change of World. Certain themes are presented here that will be developed in subsequent books. The Diamond Cutters deals with poems showing the uneasiness experienced in having to accept women's traditional roles; but there are also poems containing mosaics of personal and cultural experiences in Europe (a sort of private, inner museum), filled with "ideal landscapes", while real landscapes show the inconsistency of love, the disillusionment of romance.

Poems such as "The Platform" and "Autumn Equinox" reveal themes that will continue to be presented in the following books. In "Autumn Equinox" Rich presents a woman past her middle-age who ponders over her existence as a professor's wife; throughout the years, an utterly normal distance between husband and wife has filled her quotidian events. The woman's thoughts yield to her tedium: she finds her dissatisfactions inscribed in the outside world of autumn. "The Perennial Answer" will expose emptiness, death both of and in marriage, and the rigidity of sex roles, a central theme that appears later in the "The Phenomenology of Anger" (Rich, 1973), written some fifteen years later.
The title poem, "The Diamond Cutters", is a good example of the still very detached tone and perspective the poet uses as textual strategy; Rich explains metaphorically the craft of poetry as she conceived it in those years:

> However legendary,
> The stone is still a stone
> ...
> Now, you intelligence
> So late dredged up from dark
> Upon whose smoky walls
> Bison took fumbling form
> Or flint was edged on flint--
> Now, careful arriviste,
> Delineate at will
> Incisions in the ice.
> (Rich, 1975:31-32)

After a silence of eight years, Rich published her third book, Snapshots of a Daughter-in-Law: Poems, 1954-1962 (1963).

Snapshots of a Daughter-in-Law

Here she develops new poetic forms and begins a search for truth, her own, and her identity in her relationships with parents, husband, children, and with culture. While the poem that gives name to the book deals thematically with the daughter-in-law's personal experiences and with her confrontation with culture, it presents her tensions, frustrations and attempts to understand and name the core of her anger through the speaker's indirect rendering of experience. The woman is "she" and not "I". However, it is important to underline that Rich begins to rid her poetry of formal strategies and to speak more directly about herself. Poet and *persona* are still separated in the texts, yet this book is a transition from poems *about* experiences to poems that *are* experiences, to paraphrase Rich's own words (in Gelpi, 1975:89). Significantly, from Snapshots Rich starts dating her poems, as a way to record her own awareness and the process of becoming conscious of her inner changes. Some of the poems, such as "The Loser" (1958), and "Eurycla's Tale" (1958), are spoken by an explicit *persona*. In "The Loser" she writes from a man's point of view. The poem carries the following epigraph: "A man thinks of the woman he once loved: first, after the wedding, and then nearly a decade later" (Rich, 1963:15).

The book adds new dimensions to her poetry by showing female experience and female vision as the center of the poet's concern. Particularly important - a fact which has been stressed by critics - is the long poem in ten sections "Snapshots of a Daughter-in-Law" (1958-1960), where she polemizes against pre-conceptions, traditional values and institutions, narrating the experience from a woman's point of view: "You", "she", "a woman" are the actresses of the drama, never an "I":

> Well,
> she's long about her coming, who must be
> more merciless to herself than history
> (1963:24)

With this crucial poem she will begin to develop the process of "re-writing" and re-visioning other women authors, such as Emily Dickinson and Mary Wollstonecraft, and polemizing with writers such as Baudelaire, Dr. Johnson, Donne, and Western literary tradition in general. Rich's wide variety of readings is a constant presence in Snapshots, with poems full of allusions to art, science, literature and intertextual crossings with her poetic tradition. Man will steadily become the transgressor, the conqueror, the ruler, the opressor, clad in armor as in "The Knight" (1957), a text in which he appears as the victimizer and the victim of his own forces; the woman stands in permanent conflict between her awareness of selfhood, and the meshes of patriarchy and society trying to entangle her consciousness [3]; this conflict provides the nucleus and point of departure in her subsequent books.

Necessities of Life

If with Snapshots Rich continues to analyze woman's experience, Necessities of Life: Poems, 1962-1965 (1966) portrays her struggle to survive as a woman on her own terms. She refuses victimization, and observes sharply her own family life: the relationships with the children, and her husband. "Night-Pieces: For a Child", "The Crib", "Her Waking" show no idealization.

The ambiguities and ambivalences of these family retalionships are also to be found in Of Woman Born: Motherhood as Experience and Institution (1976a), a prose book on her personal experience as a mother and on the meaning of motherhood in pre-patriarchal and patriarchal societies. The book is a wide-ranging and an original consideration of the experience and the institution of motherhood, centered on the ideas that for a woman her body and mind are inseparable, and that control over body and mind is the primary goal for woman to begin creating her own meaning in culture. The basis for that woman-identified culture is to be found in ancient matriarchy, in the critical view of motherhood under patriarchy, and in a woman-oriented analysis of the history of obstetrics. This is, according to Rich, the basis of the struggle against woman's oppression.

In her method of exposition of Necessities of Life, Rich proves that feminist creative texts and theory can be and are to be grounded on personal materials and personal experience: letters, journals, accounts of her own life and the lives of other women, aspects that, she posits, were previously dismissed as source of information in the patriarchal system of studies. This method will become a crucial trategy in her poetry in the 1980's. Necessities of Life is a book bout experience. The poet stands close to life, and adopts from the start a desire to deal with the common and the substantial. The poem that gives the title to the volume is absolutely clear: "Piece by piece I seem/to re-enter the world: I first began/a small, fixed dot, still see/that old myself" (Rich, 1966:9). It is also important to stress that the "I" is the source of reflections, tensions, splittings. There are neither ambiguities nor formal strategies to hide the self.

Other poems in the book are overtly feminist: "I am in Danger -Sir-" (p. 33) openly criticizes the misconceptions about Emily Dickinson. This poem is the first of a series of "pictures" on notable women, which will be the particularity of A Dream of a Common Language (1978) and A Wild Patience Has Taken Me This Far (1981). In her poems on women (Mme. Curie, Caroline Hershel, Paula Becker and Clara Weshoff and Elvira Shatayev among others), Rich (1978, 1981a) reinterprets and re-creates what she envisions as their reality. In her re-interpretation of Emily Dickinson in Necessities she polemizes against Thomas Wentworth Higginson and others who considered the New England poet "half-cracked" or eccentric. Rich, in contrast, describes Dickinson in a positive way, explaining the isolation and withdrawal of the nineteenth century poet as a conscious decision to "have it out at last/on (her) own premises" (Rich, 1966:33).

There is yet another poem that belongs to the cycle of Necessities but, it was not published until the 1975 volume Poems: Selected and New. This text, "To Judith, Taking Leave", like "Roots" will later be explained as a love poem to another woman. In an interview with Elly Bulkin in Conditions, Adrienne Rich said: "When I wrote that, I didn't think of it as a lesbian poem ... But my dismissing it was akin to my dismissing the relationship, although in some ways I did not dismiss it" (Bulkin, 1977a:64).

Leaflets

With Leaflets: Poems 1965-1968 (1969), Rich emerges as an activist, fighting with her poems against an unjust society, involved in the

Civil Rights and anti-war movements of the 1960's. She now clearly articulates the oppression of women through her awareness of the patriarchal nature of power structures. If in Necessities personal relations are worked out against a background of modern chaos - destruction of cities, annihilation, garbage, disorder, decay - in Leaflets the concern is with racism, war, political repression, the destruction of nature, the abuse of language. The political invades her private life and causes despair: in "Jerusalem" (1969:23) for example, she dreams her son is riding to the war; in "Night Watch" (p. 26) her nightmare is that her husband is taken away in Hitler's death cars. If communication between men and women fails, she believes, it is due to the political and social breakdown. All have to play their new roles: "A new/era is coming in./Gauche as we are, it seems/we have to play our part" (Rich, 1966:19). The public is the private in this book, and impulses from the exterior world transform the inner vision.

In the first part of Leaflets, "Night-Watch" contains a series of poems on the private *persona* (the inner self) in a re-awakening and becoming aware of the outside world. At times, the inner self is split, as in "Orion" (p. 11), a poem addressed to the constellation, a "fierce half-brother"; the "male" constellation gives her a surge of strength. The life of men and women together begins to fail. "In The Evening" (p. 15), the man and the woman are "archaic figures", "shivering here in the half-dark 'sixties".

In other poems she also makes historical references, as in "Charleston in the Eighteen-Sixties" (p. 25), derived from the diaries of Mary Boykin Chestnut. Rich juxtaposes the romanticized images of a garden, with musings about love, and thoughts about the cruelty of death. Here, the Southern Belle does not accept the false consolation of believing that her lovers, killed in the Civil War of 1861-1865, "all dead of wounds/or blown to pieces", are now heroes:

> I'm writing, blind with tears of rage.
> In vain. Years, death, depopulation, fears,
> bondage - these shall all be borne.
> No imagination to forestall woe.
> (Rich, 1969:25)

In another poem, "Picnic" (p. 36) Rich uses images of scattered bones, of death folded in her pocket, of the coldness of rocks to shatter the idyllic setting. The short poem relies on intonational effects, produced by the absence of punctuation to provoke the contrast between a "normal" situation, which should be one of contentment, and the imminent presence of "ice", coldness, death.

The second part of *Leaflets* takes a more active way toward the external world, particularly in the sequence "Ghazals: Homage to Ghalib", in which the poet openly polemizes with the notion that history is repetition; neither old wisdom nor old experience will help to deal with contemporary life. This long poem, a series of seventeen written from August 12, to September 8, 1968, was inspired by Rich's own translation of Ghalib, done for Aijaz Ahmad, editor of the *Ghazals*. Rich felt strong parallels between her times and those of the Arabic poets'. She identifies with Ghalib, yet with a certain distance, for she begins to discover language as a constantly changing medium of subjective expression. For this reason, there is no such thing as an objective vision: "When they read this poem of mine, they are translators./Every existence speaks a language of its own" (p.75). Thus in the introductory notes to the poems she wrote: "My ghazals are personal and public, American and twentieth-century; but they owe much to the presence of Ghalib in my mind" (p. 59).

Rich adapted the Ghazal form, keeping the five couplet structure in non-prosodic meter, each couplet conceived as a juxtaposition of images which are also related and interwoven with the rest. In these associations, Rich's image of lovers is linked with those of prisoners, soldiers, students, political activists; her ghazals speak the language of the times. It is the lexicon of arrests, graffiti, censorship, of unrest in the North-American city whose inhabitants are disillusioned in a world where there is no justice, no order, for this is "an age of political and cultural break-up". In an essay in 1973 she explicitly writes that the bombings in Indochina are "acts of concrete sexual violence, an expression of the congruence of violence and sex in the masculine psyche" (Rich, 1979c:109). Other poems in the book, such as "To Frantz Fanon" (p. 43), indicate her sympathies with the Martinican-born revolutionary and with his indictments to the United States as imperialistic. <u>Leaflets</u> as Rich herself writes, was inspired by Paul Goodman's <u>Drawing the Line</u> and by Simone Weil's books (Rich, 1969:79). This volume, as well as <u>The Will to Change: Poems, 1968-1970</u> (1971), her following book, contain several political poems, among them "For a Russian Poet", "Implosions", "Ghazals", "Study of History", "The Burning of Paper Instead of Children".

The Will to Change

In <u>The Will to Change</u> (1971) the poet continues to explore the private and the public, particularly concerning the way language affects both public and private experiences. As in her previous book, the verse breaks barriers between poetry and prose; it is, at times colloquial. Rich makes wide use of images from the visual arts, music, science and philosophy to explore the self and to speak to other women. Of particular relevance is the poem "Planetarium" (Rich, 1971:13-14), a dialogue between the woman-poet, and the woman-astronomer Caroline Herschel, both being part of the world of "galaxies of women". This is a meta-poem about the process by which the speaker and *persona* become one: it begins with the astronomer as seen by the speaker, and its closure makes it evident that speaker and object of vision are one:

> A woman in the shape of a monster
> a monster in the shape of a woman
> the skies are full of them
> ...
> I am an instrument in the shape
> of a woman trying to translate pulsations
> into images for the relief of the body
> and the reconstruction of the mind
> (p. 14)

Other poems, such as "Pierrot Le Fou" (pp. 25-28), "Images of Godard" (pp. 47-49) explore the city as metaphor of language, a <u>locus</u> the poet captures visually. "The Blue Ghazals", a series of nine poems dated from September 21, 1968 to May 4, 1969, in dialogue with the previous "Ghazals", records the relationship between a man, a woman, and a city: the city is filth and chaos, violence, all caused by man:

> A man, a woman, a city.
> The city as object of love,
>
> Anger and filth in the basement.
> The furnace stoked and blazing.
>
> A sexual heat in the pavements.
> (Rich, 1971:21)

The city will continue to be more and more a space of violation, anger, corruption. In The Will to Change, the image of the male figure recurs by a metonymic relation, to represent male power, the authorities, the government, well portrayed in poems suchs as "I Dream I'm the Death of Orpheus" (p. 19) and "Meditations for a Savage Child" (1973:53).

The title of the book quotes a line from Charles Olson's "The King Fishers": "What does not change/is the will to change", but she explores change on her own premises. The title poem, written between 1969-1970, is a text in five sections, a collage of topics dedicated to various persons, where Rich freely intertwines the political and the public, stressing the lack of freedom even in those artists who speak about freedom. Rich makes politics personal by incorporating her own experience as a woman and a poet with the political consciousness of woman's place in society. Politics and war are seen as menaces to the world because they represent male power. Now the city is also the victim of the drama:

> The cabdriver from the Bronx
> screaming: "This city's GOTTA die!"
>
> dynamiting it hourly from his soul
> as surely as any terrorist
> (Rich, 1971:44)

There is "the will" to change, and Adrienne Rich's next books - Driving into the Wreck: Poems, 1971-1972 (1973), A Dream of a Common Language: Poems, 1974-1977 (1978), and A Wild Patience Has Taken Me

<u>This Far: Poems, 1978-1981</u> (1981) - explore the world of women in a polemical attitude against institutions and culture. As she wrote in <u>Leaflets</u>: "Did you think I was talking about my life?/I was trying to drive a tradition up against the wall" (p. 64).

This forward stance of Rich's language, particularly in contrast with her early modes of expression where the poet's world vision was consistently veiled by the ornament of the poetic device, irritated some critics especially those who expected her to continue writing poems that "are neatly and modestly dressed, that speak quiet but do not mumble", (Auden, 1975:127). By way of example, according to Robert Boyers, <u>Leaflets</u> shows a "decline" in Rich's career, because of what he considers "reflections of a will to be contemporary", and, he goes on to contend on "how charged she has become with the nauseous propaganda of the advance-guard cultural radicals", and he concludes that Rich "is neither a radical innovator nor the voice of an age" (1973: 156-157). A decade later these words would only be part of the history of the reception of Rich's early work. Subsequently, various readings of the poet's creative production after <u>The Will to Change</u> and <u>Diving into the Wreck</u> have led many critics to interpret her work as a close exploration of the relationship between poetry and patriarchy.

<u>Driving into the Wreck</u>

Elaborating on Rich's idea of the androgyne in the title poem of <u>Diving</u>, and echoing Helen Vendler's phrase which refers to Rich's poems as "dispatches from the battlefield" (Vendler, 1973:170), Erica Jong writes: "This stranger-poet-survivor carries 'a book of myths' in which her/his 'names do not appear'. These are the old myths of patriarchy, the myths that split male and female irreconciliably into two warring factions, the myths that perpetuate the battle between the sexes", (Jong, 1975:174).

In fact, in "The Phenomenology of Anger", a central poem in <u>Diving</u>, a woman tryingly and disjointly speaks out the reasons for her female anger, in an attempt to understand the process she is undergoing: the act of becoming conscious of her lack of freedom, of man's love for violence and war, of the world outside she feels alienated from and that she has no wish to join as she sees it. The mistrust of the "male" world and of the language of patriarchy is a key point in this poem, indeed in the entire book. Now Rich's open stance is against "the oppressor's language", as she had written earlier in "The Burning of Paper Instead of Children" (1968) and in "Our Whole Life" (1969), both from The Will to Change. Thus in "The Phenomenology of Anger" the speaker's final realization is that she "would have loved to live in a world/of women and men gaily/in collusion with green leaves, ..." (Rich, 1973:30). But this is an impossibility and it remains an utopia. After analyzing her own reality and her experience with respect to the external world, the woman recalls:

> *"The only real love I have ever felt*
> *was for children and other women,*
> *Everything else was lust, pity,*
> *self-hatred, pity lust".*
> This is a woman's confession ...
> (p. 30)

Yet not every hope is lost. It is in this period when Rich cherishes the idea of "androgyny" as the answer to make of the world a better one. Such are the key images in "The Stranger" and "Diving into the Wreck" both dated 1972.

In "The Stranger" Rich insightfully shows a new line between poetry and patriarchy. Speaking in the first person singular, in the persona of the androgyne, the poet unfolds a synecdochical voice for both male and female (Stimpson, 1980:187). The androgyny is a transition between an attempt to find meaning in life with the world of men, and the need to identify with women. As a transitional text, "The Stranger" indicates that definitions of sex and gender are unstable; according to Rich, the acceptance of androgyny is a way of redeeming herself. The compelling dream here - the utopia - is that of an androgynous society, in the sense of people living in a genderless system in which one's sexual identity should not be a determinant factor for socio-cultural conditions.

In the title poem of <u>Diving into the Wreck</u>, Rich develops images of divers (from J. Cousteau films), and examines the "wreck" produced by patriarchal values, finally to contemplate herself both as a mermaid and a merman (the two comprising the androgyny). In "The Stranger" the androgyny was a state of mind; in "Diving" the merman and the mermaid's represent the new nature of the man-woman relationship, and the wish that the subconscious find its truth in a unified being. The idea of androgyny, which seemed to her the solution for the ideal of being in 1972 and 1973, is abandoned as theme in her next three books. In 1976, Rich looks back on this concept, and refuses to adopt it because now it has acquired another meaning: "It's essentially the notion that the male will somehow incorporate into himself female attributes - tenderness, gentleness, ability to cry, to feel, to express, not to be rigid. But what does it mean for women? ... I don't think of androgyny as progress any more, I think it is a useless term ..." (Bulkin, 1977a:62). She then affirms the reconstruction of the woman's world within the framework of women's relationships never losing touch with the roads to find her identity. Adrienne Rich's indefatigable search takes her even further than the answers she could obtain. Never to stop knowing the world, Rich writes in 1982:

> I mean knowing the world, and my place in it, not
> in order to stare with bitterness or detachment,
> but as a powerful and womanly series of choices:
> and here I write the words, in their fullness:
> powerful;   womanly.
>
> (Rich, 1983:35)

I.2. READING AND WRITING AS RE-VISION AND PROGRAM

In the 1970's, with the publication of The Will to Change, Diving into the Wreck and the essays "When We Dead Awaken: Writing as Re-Vision" (1971) and "The Anti-Feminist Woman" (1972), Adrienne Rich opened new areas of meaning for feminist discourse, a fact which engendered or provoked an important change in the state of affairs of the current criticism on her work. Indeed from that period there is a clearly distinguishable split among the critics of her work: those who accept her texts and her ways of approaching language, and those who reject this and who therefore do not attempt to read her following her own codes, and do not interpret the transformations as part of an on-going process, dismissing her for being too polemical, a feminist, or lesbian (Bulkin, 1977a; 1977b; Cf. Clemons, 1975; Brown; Vendler, 1981).

With Erica Jong's and Wendy Martin's essays in 1973, we witness the beginning of feminist criticism focusing on Rich's poetry and the work of other in the way Rich herself suggests as "re-vision". In the article "From Patriarchy to the Female Principle", Martin (1975:175-188) shows how a chronological reading of the poet's work records that struggle. In fact, we would add to Martin's analysis that Rich wishes to re-write and re-read the history of women, revealing them in their true nature, and exposing the ways in which society oppresses them.

It is quite instructive to consider other aspects related to the different modes of existence of feminist discourse especially in what concerns important dates of publication. Between 1960 and 1968 Anne Sexton, H.D., Sylvia Plath, Denise Levertov, Diane Wakoski and Adrienne Rich had each produced at least one volume of poetry which would pave the way for what we know nowadays as feminist poetic discourse. It is our belief that Adrienne Rich's essay "When We Dead Awaken: Writing as Re-Vision", from 1971, together with her subsequent articles, have been one of the keystones in the shaping of contemporary women's discourse, be it feminist or lesbian/feminist. Those were times, no doubt, of mutual encouragement among writers, critics, and readers as well. It is no mere coincidence that in 1973 the first important anthologies of the decade appear, such as No More Masks! An Anthology of Poems by Women, edited by Florence Howe and Ellen Bass, Rising Tides: 20th Century American Women Poets, edited by Laura Chester and Sharon Barba, and Psyche: The Feminine Poetic Conciousness, in an edition by Barbara Segnitz and Carol Rainey. In 1974 Louise Bernikow edited The World Split Open: Four Centuries of Women Poets in England and America, 1552-1950. Since then the list of anthologies has continued to grow. Needless to say, there were other developments of anthropological, psychological, historical, linguistic, literary feminist thinking concomitant to the rising of a wider circulation of poetic texts.

The practice of feminist writing expands. Soon the poetic production brings about new female-oriented imagery and themes deviating from traditional tenets. Most importantly, this type of discourse is carried forward through a re-affirmation of the need to push language relentlessly beyond the limits of patriarchy. It is evident that it is Rich's notion of *revision* that first pointed the itinerary of feminist oriented aesthetics in poetic discourse. Language can no longer be a neutral medium. Writing and language must be the space and the instruments to shape an ideology that only begins to be reified and named. In the light of this schema, Rich's poetry is a journey from verbal art to a poetic discourse in which the feminist factor will be the element of primary components around which the other elements will be actualized.

In Adrienne Rich's earlier poems the verbal art is made manifest in the choice of specific combinations of words at a semantic as well as a phonological level subordinated to the aesthetic project of the *generic* poetic discourse of the major North-American poets in the 1950's - which, for example, won Rich the praise of W.H. Audèn. The progressive movement is also one from writing as a *poet* to writing as a *female* poet and whose choice of elements in her artistic texts - rhythm, occasional rhyme, internal division of lines, intonational, phonological elements, similes, metaphors - even the separation between poetry and prose, will now be subordinated to and oriented towards a communicative function. That is, Rich's poetry becomes a mode of textual production that is not only or not *specifically* aesthetic. No longer will Adrienne Rich shape her voice in such strict prosodic patterns where form predominates. The closural stanza of "Why Else But to Forestall This Hour" is self-explanatory:

> I am the man who has outmisered death,
> In pains and cunning laid my seasons by.
> Now I must toil to win each hour and breath;
> I am too full of years to reason why.
> (Rich, 1975:5)

Words will no longer be used exclusively as components of aesthetic interaction. The poet will therefore direct the reader's attention to aspects of her language and world-vision in ways she did not emphasize before.

Rich's own concept of "re-vision" became more than an inspiration; it became a kind of program to follow in the future. This is somehow a circular phenomenon, a process of mutual enrichment between the poet and those who set in motion, through valorization, the given discourse. On the one hand, inspired and programmed by the texts subject to analysis, the feminist approach to literary criticism found in Rich's poetry and prose a source of insight and a program which it could apply. On the other hand, Adrienne Rich discovered new possibilities of evolution in her work: "By the time of the women's movement I already had a body of work, more or less recognized by the establishment. But the women's movement connected for me with the conflicts and concerns I'd been feeling when I wrote 'Snapshots of a Daughter-in-Law'" (Buikin, 1977a:51). In 1971 Rich wrote in "When We Dead Awaken":

> Re-vision - the act of looking back, of seeing
> with fresh eyes, of entering an old text from a
> new critical direction - is for us more than a
> chapter in cultural history: it is an act of survival.

In this often quoted and important passage, and in the text that follows it, Adrienne Rich concentrates on several aspects that are fundamental to a feminist approach to literature. She posits the need for woman's own identity, and the need to survive by rescuing a culture that is still to be discovered. Furthermore, Rich cautions against tradition which is dominated by patriarchy. She does so not for the simple reason of giving a warning, but to induce feminist criticism to undertake a re-vision of that tradition in order to understand woman's situation in a society which is and has been male-oriented. Along with this, Rich provides the perspective from which to evaluate and read what is *already known*, and suggests guidelines for a thematic orietation in the study and creative impulse of woman's writing and criticism, a project to define and direct woman's search for knowledge within a major cultural sphere whose language "has trapped as well as liberated" them.

Adrienne Rich begins her own re-vision through fresh consideration of her readings of American poets who are her contemporaries, as a way to sift the feminist quality from the feminine. Thus, her readings of Sylvia Plath and Diane Wakoski (Rich, 1979b:36) reveal that "in the work of both Man appears as, if not a dream, a fascination and a terror; and that the source of the fascination and the terror is, simply, Man's power - to dominate, tyranize, choose, or reject the woman". Likewise, her new consideration of Sappho, Christina Rossetti, Emily Dickinson, H.D., Ann Bradstreet and others brings her an awareness of the ambivalnce with which she used to read them (p. 93), as well as a fresh valorization.

Rich therefore focuses more and more on the communicative function of language in her prose for the re-vision of the language she is trying to create. In her poetry blank verse disappears, yet she still uses rhythmic elements of non-metrical prosody now with more emphasis so that these intonational components serve an emphatic purpose in the expression of her ideas, and in the equally important development of images. "For writers, and at this moment for women writers in particular, there is the challenge and promise of a whole new psychic geography to be explored", (Rich, 1979b:35), she affirms, linking the act of re-vision with the specific relationship of women's creativity, language, and images for "a consciousness we are just coming into, and with little in the past to support us" (Rich, 1979b:35).

I.3. THE MAKING OF AN IDEOLOGY

In 1971 Rich Suggested a specifically feminist approach to traditional discourse. Six years later, in her essay "The Meaning of Our Love for Women is What We Have Constantly to Expand", (1977b) she describes the direction lesbian/feminist writing is undertaking under the hands of North-American women who are taking new risks through the pages of different literary journals, a direction which provides an accurate synthesis of her textual strategies in The Dream of a Common Language (1978) and A Wild Patience Has Taken Me This Far (1981): "These women, and many like them, are trying to reveal and express and support our female complexity; acting *towards* rather than *against;* moving us forward" (Rich, 1977b:7). Thus Rich - speaking from her lesbian/feminist position - is no longer reacting predominantly against the world of patriarchy, but is acting towards the meaning and complexities of bonds and alliances among women, moving into the nurturing world these relationships can create. If man exists in this new type of discourse, it is only incidentally, as a distant presence, as an outsider to this woman's world, or as a transgressor, and, ironically, as a deterritorialized being.

If silence, estrangement, rage were instilled into or attributed to women in the past, now is the occasion to reverse roles and to destroy stereotypes. Man, children, women themselves are silhouetted upon a broader disc of relations, feelings, and sensations. Man may have stamped his presence as friend, lover, as a literary tradition, as a ruler of language. The poet splits off from that world, and projects herself away into the woman-to-woman world, where man's language will no longer reach the speaker.

A myriad of ne impressions are cast upon the reader. The speaker in those poems no longer dwells in a world of conventions and institutions. Out of a freshly conceived realm of women Rich re-constructs the possibilities for a new, different world. Therefore the emphasis falls upon something hitherto ignored, on unsuspected visions. At last the speaker accustoms herself to twilight and discerns the shape of things - in ways that are profound and truer to the inner voices of her identity, pointing her truths with precision. In a comforting and humane tone, the speaker's voice, again and again, finds new ways of proving that truth is to be explored within the domain of female silence.

Both The Dream of a Common Language and A Wild Patience Has Taken Me This Far are further developments from her first irritations with the conventional world, which, although dispersed at the beginning, became inevitable. These two books contextualize woman-to-woman relations in North-American culture, another stage in Adrienne Rich's conscious act of creation and re-creation.

The Dream does not provide a "common language" but suggests its foundations. In this book Rich proposes the need to re-construct language by introducing new codes in order to build a new system of correlations for women in society. As she writes in the poem "Origins and History of Consciousness" (1970-1974), the true nature of poetry is "the drive to connect;" later she will state: "Poetry is above all a concentration of the *power* of language, which is the power of our ultimate relationship to everything in the universe" (Rich, 1979g:248). This, however, also implies the necessity to live in constant suspicion of words, even of one's own, in suspicion of discourse itself, and of the uses of discourse by women themselves.

The poet in Rich directs the reader, by means of her textual strategies, in this act of cooperation. The reader, in turn, controls the selections and actualizes the ideological structures suggested by and incorporated into the text. Rich's poetic language is no longer a neutral medium that passes freely into the private craft of the speaker's intentions. It becomes inhabited by the intentions and readings of others. Briefly speaking, this is the change of Rich's poetic discourse from the *verbal art* to the creation of aesthetic texts with a very important communicative function as well. [4]

Since the 1970's Rich's discourse - both poetic and critical - has been expanded by liberal feminists in the United States. After the publication of some of her essays and prose (Rich, 1976a; 1977a; 1979a; 1980) and of the <u>Twenty-One-Love Poems</u> (1976a), it has become an important instrument for radical lesbian feminists. It is the feminists who assume the various subject-functions of Rich's discourse, and it is precisely this readership the one which gives existence to her discourse. This is not surprising; on the publication of the above mentioned love poems, we gather the following: "Effie's Press seemed like a very natural place to publish it. I wanted it in women's hands" (Bulkin, 1977a:59). [5] In the course of three decades, not only the criticism but also the readership of Rich's work has become more and more specifically women, at the same time that the focus of commentaries on her poetry has shifted its ground from stylistic achievement and imagistic developments to thematic aspects.

What I have called "the appropriation" - in quite a positive connotative sense - of Rich's discourse by feminist writers, critics, and readers is the consequence of a common purpose to expose patriarchal power, to perform a critique of former representations of gender and women in all possible areas of discourse, especially those areas of writing which have been, up to now, repressed. This position is what initiates the "political" grounds of feminist writing. The notions of "private" and "political" are still part of working definitions and hypotheses in contemporary criticism. Yet, we can rightly say that given Rich's critique of society, her poetry represents an integration of the private and the political, a quality several male writers of the twentieth century have shared - Osip Mandelstam, Vladimir Mayakovsky, César Vallejo, and Pablo Neruda - to mention just a few.

However, almost no women are known to have been seen from this perspective before the rise of feminist literature in the United States. Even though our subject of discussion in the present study is neither the definitions nor the introduction of a typology of the private and political in poetry, it is important to mention that parallel to the development of feminist poetry in the United States, led primarily by white Americans, the emergence of Black women poets introduces new dimensions of the private and the political because in these voices, race, class, and sexuality appear most often interwined in the individual.[6]

The political property of Rich's poetic discourse in the last decade is characterized by an ideological component. That is to say, Rich's poetry is both an aethetic and an ideological discourse. It is aesthetic in that it is self-referential, aiming at an aesthetic effectiveness. By the ideological quality of a given discourse, a fundamental component of Rich's poetry from the 1970's, we understand the systematic making of a poetic argument which follows a body of premises - implicit of explicit - and brings to a common center a specific area of a given semantic field. Inevitably, this mode of argument is only a part within the Global Semantic System comprising all spheres of a given culture, including the patriarchal and non-patriarchal spheres.[7] It is in this sense that we can state that the search for a foundation of a world in which women are given predominant importance represents the mode of argument of radical lesbian/feminist ideology. The Dream, A Wild Patience, and Rich's essay on "Compulsory Heterosexuality and Lesbian Existence" (1980) corroborate this.

This ideological property, however, is not a constant in her poetry for it applies only to the consciously programmatic discourse in her work from the 1970's as we have previously discussed. It should also be stressed that the thematic development of her poetry is a movement from a strictly detached, non-committed stand in 1951 to the systematic creation a world-vision and a particular criticism of society through language. This results in the building up of an ideological and poetic discourse emerging as a necessary and alternative world and ideology in polemic relation, opposed to the one already existing.

The method used by Rich to develop arguments in her poetry and her essays is the *performance of a displacement of connotations*. As she explains in the answer to an inquiry on the word "lesbian":

> Since the word itself was not current until the

> turn of the century, and since its connotations
> have been loaded with so much negativity, I feel
> comfortable reclaiming the word retroactively, as
> it were.
> (Schwarz, 1979:4; cf. Rich, 1980:650)

Not just the word itself, but especially the contextual connotations are being reclaimed. Quite interestingly, in <u>The Dream of a Common Language</u> the word "lesbian" is not mentioned, yet this book reveals multiple contexts of related semantic fields. Rich avoids the mention of the word yet the poems in that book are a major metaphor to reclaim its meaning.[8] The ideological operation the poet is performing can be illustrated by the following componential analysis which serves as paradigm for the multiple displacements that can be applied (we borrow the model from Geckeler, 1976; Eco, 1979, and place it in our own context):

A. Patriarchal concept of human relationships:

    WOMAN TO WOMAN---LESBIAN---DEVIANT---UNDESIRABLE = (-)

    WOMAN TO MAN---HETEROSEXUAL---NORMAL---DESIRABLE = (+)

B. Rich's new correspondences and oppositions:

    WOMAN TO WOMAN---LESBIAN---NORMAL---------DESIRABLE = (+)

    WOMAN TO MAN---HETEROSEXUAL---DEVIANT---UNDESIRABLE = (-)

The ideological displacement of emotional connotations of negativity is done from A to B as shown in the diagram, indicated by the movement of the markers "normal" and "deviant" (Cf. Rich, 1980). This is especially true and evident in <u>The Dream</u> and <u>A Wild Patience</u>.

Consider, for example, the lines "women, deviants, witnesses ..." (Rich, 1978:27); those are women outside the law, not just the women of the twentieth century, but also women from the past, as the poem "Heroines" suggests (Rich, 1981a:33): "Exceptional/even deviant/you draw your long skirts/across the nineteenth century". It should be noted that this operation is being performed not just by direct mention of the word (e.g. "lesbian", "deviant") but by the creation of contexts as in the totality of the subjects of both books, where it is not only a single word taken retroactively, but the multiplicity of possible semantic fields connected with the definitions of relationships among women, the connections of women and society, woman and nature. From this follows the need to create if not a new language, then a language devoid of the negativity directed to women, a language that is different, even from the one women themselves use. As Rich writes: "For many women, the commonest words are having to be sifted through, rejected, laid aside for a long time, or turned to the light for new colors and flashes of meaning: *power, love, control, violence, political, personal, private, friendship, community, sexual, work, pain, pleasure, self, integrity* ..." (Rich, 1979g:247). In other words, we can say that to Rich, discourse should not only be used to explore the world of women (as a way to enlarge the universe of discourse in general) but should also serve the purpose of shifting the negativity attributed to every crucial word being used in feminist and lesbian texts. This is one of the major aethetic elements brought in by contemporary feminist discourse: a new mode of self-referentiality.

The feminist reader absorbs the meaning of Rich's poetic discourse into her existence and amalgamates the topics of many of the poems into her own subjectivity. Within the *spectrum* of the *author function* and its "concrete" reader or audience, Rich's discourse has been pathbreaking. If in the last years feminist critics have centered their own discourse more and more on the ideas in Rich's poetry, it is because Rich herself has directed the readers in that direction, not just through her essays and articles, but also in the textual strategies themselves. She has designed in her texts the type of interpretations she envisions. At the same time the she consciously wants to deprogram the former ideological structures that have shaped women's consciousness in the past- the male oriented frames. In short, she is criticizing the old system of thoughts, the past tradition, while trying to build a new ideological framework to understand women's attitudes and psyche. She is, of course, not alone in her endeavor, for other feminist writers and critics, such as Kate Millett (1970) in the critique of fiction, Mary Daly (1978) in prose, and Susan Griffin

(1978) and Judy Grahn (1978) in poetry, also begin to do a similar process in other areas.

The discourse of Adrienne Rich is the expression of a reconstruction both of the received hierarchies of literature and society, and of pre-established assumptions; it is sustained by the ideological framework we have previously discussed. It is precisely that framework what makes of Rich's poetry an exception in the context of the United States. Muriel Rukeyser and Denise Levertov have also developed in their poetry a "personal awakening to political and social life, and situate their consciousness and its formation as a specific historical moment" (Du Plessis, 1979a:280). Susan Griffin has explored the political/private in women by focusing on the relationship of mother and daughter, on woman and Nature. Judy Grahn, as Rich herself has written, "calls up the living woman against the manufactured one, the manmade creation of centuries of male art and literature" (Rich, 1979g: 253).

Furthermore, the poets awakening to political and social life are not necessarily or exclusively of feminist orientation among women writers in the United States. A totally different *spectrum* is to be found in the works of Black-North-American women poets from 1960 to the present. Their writing is the search and struggle for change within the dominant system, and for the recovery of a shattered culture. But the quest for identity and the need to re-territorialize women by means of language is different from the white feminist poets' own search.

We may agree with Rachel Blau Du Plessis (1979:280) that "In poems about women, politics and war, and myth the poets (Rich, Rukeyser, and Levertov) construct critiques of culture and ideology from a radical and often feminist point of view. The act of critique guides the central acts of perception in the poems". However, neither in Rukeyser nor in Levertov do we find the postulates and the *poetic argument* structuring their poetry within a *system of ideological structures processed in the course of writing* and of its development, as we find it in Rich. While there are certain broad features which not only Rukeyser, Rich, and Levertov have in common - and together with them many other contemporary American poets - the way in which they make use of words differs, their purposes do not often coincide, and their methods are dissimilar. Therefore each poet needs to be approached by the reader correspondingly according to each poet's textual strategies, and in each one's own *author-function spectrum*.

To conclude, by her utilization of a "common" language echoing Wordsworth's "Preface" to the Lyrical Ballads, Adrienne Rich aims at creating poetry against rhetoric, at disowning the lying figures of speech, the disguise of form, the masks of poetic diction, and instead, proposes a critically and an emotionally charged language of common life. However, unlike Wordsworth's notion of "common language" in the life of men, Rich's common language is the medium of expression aimed at collective and ordinary experience, a common language *for women* and *by women*. Her poetry, in polemic against Wordworth's concept, is a counterforce to the authoritative and the dominant discourses, to the tradition of patriarchal power, to that power which literature as an institution has received and delivered. The first poem of The Dream of a Common Language, titled "Power" (Rich, 1978:3) is highly representative of the dialectic notion of Rich's ideology: woman's power originates in the same source as her wounds. Thus in the critique of received hierarchies and the transvaluation of received judgements and assumptions, we find this dialectics applied in women's discourse as well. It is within this framework that Rich's activity of *author-function* should be understood.

II. THE POET AND THE ALIEN TEXT

II.1. INTERTEXTUALITY IN FEMINIST POETIC DISCOURSE

The new rise of feminist consciousness in the twentieth century has put to test the question of the women's proverbial subservience, particularly in the last three decades. For feminist writers, and poets, to work critically and creatively does not imply to perform a negation of aesthetic norms, but means to write against "the forces of the preceding codes" (Corti, 1976; Eco, 1976; Cf. Díaz-Diocaretz 1983a, 1983b), and to set forth a new social organization of their dicourse with respect to the dominant esthetic norms. For these writers, western culture is, in the words of Adrienne Rich, "a book of myths/in which/our names do not appear" (1972 in 1975:198).

This book of myth stands as metaphor, in a feminist context, for the text as sign produced by patriarchal ideology. Given this perspective, my central proposition will be the following: In the practice of a new, emancipatory feminist writing, the feminist poet reads the patriarchal text, and appropriates it to create a textual interaction. In such an interaction we can sift through the arguments of a dialogue in polemic with the varying modes of existence of patriarchal discourse. Within the dynamic *continuum* of language as a sociohistorically and ideologically changeable phenomenon (Mukarovsky, 1977), and centered in the complex relationship between the acts of reading and of writing, there is one aspect which stands out: the poet as reader of *other* texts, and as a writer herself. My notion of the poet and the alien text in feminist discourse can be equated with the idea of the feminist poet versus patriarchal corpus of texts. It should be emphasized that this interaction *from within* is far from corresponding to the distinction betwen the "woman as reader" understood as key concept for *feminist critique,* and "the woman as writer" to define *gynocritique* or *gynocritics* proposed by Elaine Showalter (1979:25).

An insight into the paradigms found in the corpus of eleven books of poetry by the North-American writer Adrienne Rich will throw light into the poetry of other women publishing since around the 1950's to the present in the United States. The aim is, eventually, to proceed back in time from the study of these poets, in order to understand the poetry by women from earlier periods by tracing some basic modes of differentiation of the uses of the alien text. In general, my interest is oriented at finding out, first of all, if feminist discourse as such actually exists, distinct from other types of discourse; second, if the latter is true, it would be necessary to discover and define what characterizes those poems written from a feminist orientation, and to assess which components are peculiar to this corpus of texts, and to what extent they are related or unrelated to a feminist consciousness as well as to the corresponding tradition.

Feminist critics of American poetry have, up to the present, mainly focused on female imagery and its characteristics in women's writing. The limited number of essays *on intertextuality* have predominantly dealt with the following: subject matter and sources in American poetry (Carruthers, 1979), mythological themes and images (Ostriker, 1982), and French literature, especially fiction (Marks, 1979). There is a need for more studies of formal elements in poetry in this context. It needs to be said that my position is one of disagreement with those who believe that language is inherently oppressive – as one area of feminist criticism contends (on this issue see, for example Spender, 1980, Cf. Black & Coward, 1981; McKluskie, 1983; also Elshtain, 1982). To analyse intertextuality as strategy is to focus particularly on how the poet breaks the monoideism and monolatry of meaning and of writing, as set by male-oriented discourse. It means, together with this, to study the textual strategies, and to explore the poet's capacity to settle in the semiotic context of a given culture, and to uncover the poet's particular forms of heterogeneity and difference. Furthermore, the reader of a feminist text receives a discourse – still in process – which may be overt on the thematic level, yet quite complex on the formal level.

In order to present the problems from another angle, I shall suggest the following questions:

1) How does the poet handle the material of the formerly existent

texts, that is, of the *already read?*

2) Since the poet's writing exists simultaneously to or after the alien texts, which unstated, unnamed critical attitude is assumed in relation to those texts before which there exists a position of privilege?

3) How is this critical attitude expressed? Is it related to the semiotic fact of excluding or including the formerly existent? Which are the paradigms of expression?

4) What elements does the poet provide or conceal to the readers for the reception of the poetic message?

5) Can we trace any formal difference, from the point of view of intertextuality, between a non-feminist, a feminist, and a lesbian text?

Before proceeding to the exposition of the material itself we shall briefly direct our attention towards the problem of terminology raised by the term *intertextuality*. It was originally established as a concept by Julia Kristeva (1968:47, 1974:59-60) who defines it as the interaction of texts produced within a single text: poetic language becomes a dialogue of texts. Each sequence functions in relation to another one whose origin is in still another text, so that the text is at the same time a reminiscence and a transformation of that other text. *Intertextualité* is proposed by Kristeva also as the phenomenon in which every text is the absorption and transformation of other texts; here, the notion of *intertextualité* comes to take the place of *intersubjectivity*. (1969:146). Later, Kristeva (1974; 1980:15, *passim*) revisions this too general concept and redefines it as the transposition of one or more systems of signs into another accompanied by a new articulation of the enunciative and denotative positions.

Jury Tynianov (1965) postulates that every literary work is built as a double layer of differential *rapports,* in the first place with the pre-existent literary texts, in the second, with non-literary systems of signification (e.g. the oral languages). Roland Barthes (1979:77), following Kristeva's notion, adds that "Every text being itself the intertext of another text, belongs to the intertextual, which must not be confused with a text's origins: to search for 'the source of' and 'influence upon' a work to satisfy the myths of filiation". From these early theoretical propositions, Gérard Genette (1979) develops some new concepts around his framework of "transtextuality", which consists of the set of relations between a text and other texts, among which he includes:

1. *Intertextuality:* the more or less literal presence of one text into another.
2. *Metatextuality:* the relation of a given text to commentaries on it.
3. *Paratextuality:* the relation of a text to imitations or transformations of it such as parodies and *pastiches*.
4. *Archtextuality:* The relation between a text and its archtext.

All these concepts, as well as their definitions were proposed without any specific interest on the concrete analysis of poetry.

Under the concept of "subtext", Kiril Taranovsky (1976) provides a classification which is useful to apply to poetic texts. The subtext is "an already existing text (or texts) reflected in a new one", and is divided in the following types:

a) That which serves as a simple impulse for the creation of an image.
b) The borrowing of a rhytmic figure and the sounds contained therein.
c) The text which supports or reveals the poetic message of a later text.
d) The text which is treated polemically by the poet. (1976:18).

These four types can be combined in different ways. For Taranovsky and the Soviet Formalists the subtext is "the source of the repeated element, not the element itself; that is, the subtext is a text which is diachronically releated to the one in question" (Rusinko, 1979:20).

Although Kristeva is known to have coined the term *intertextualité* and to have introduced it into French Structuralism, I am inclined to return to what seems to be unquestionably the starting point *in meaning*, of this concept. In the 1960's Mikhail Bakhtin was still little known in Western Europe; in <u>Le Marxisme et la Philosophie du Language</u>, dated 1929-1930 (1977:136), on the subject of what he called "verbal interaction", he writes:

> En outre, l'acte de parole sous forme de livre est toujours orienté en fonction des prises de parole antérieures dans le même sphère d'activité, tant celles de l'auteur lui-même que celles d'autres auteurs: il découle donc de la situation particulière d'un problème scientifique ou d'un style de production littéraire. Ainsi, le discours écrit est en quelque sorte partie intégrante d'une discussion idéologique à une grande échelle: il répond a quelque chose, il refute, il confime, il anticipe sur les reponses et objections potentielles, cherche un soutien, etc.

Bakhtin's theoretical suggestions have been crucial for the understanding of the juxapositions and distinctions between the modes of functioning both of the verbal art and ideology.

"L'acte de parole" in the form of a book is embedded with social existence, is part of a community as an aesthetic and cultural object. Yet this object is dynamic given the orientation of its ideological argument: responding, refuting, confirming, looking for support. And the verbal art is made through language, *via* the word, which for Bakhtin (1973:167) is the "eternally changing medium of dialogical intercourse. It never coincides with a single consciousness or a single voice". The dialogical intercourse sets the poet's subjective inner consciousness in its own dialectic. The word exists as it is transferred "from one mouth to another, one context to another, one social collective to another", from the poet to the world, from the world to the poet, in the constant interplay of the *Me* and that which is not *Me* in the poet, and speaks through a verbal art to this social collective, as an individual. In this process of transferral, Bakhtin goes on to say, "the word does not forget where it has been and can never wholly free itself from the dominion of the context of which it has been part" (1973:167).

The dwelling place of the alien text is, then, *where it has been, and the contexts of which it has been part*. The poet and the alien text are two discoursive entities in dialectic and dialogical interrelationship. We can call *alien text* (Cf. "alien word", Lotman, 1976) all textual manifestations of another text, whether external (rapport of one text to another) or internal (rapport of a text with itself) (Ricardou, 1971:162), explicit or implicit (Jenny, 1976), and restricted intertextuality (intertextual relations among texts by the same author) (Dällenbach, 1976:282). The alien text represents the text(s) that comes to constitute – as a sign of an entire message or part of it – what is not peculiar to the text in question. In a feminist context, the patriarchal text represents authoritative discourse (a term I borrow from Bakhtin, 1973) which is the privileged language that approaches us not from within, but from without.

The feminist intertextual factor consists of an act of displacement of this privileged word "which no longer speaks, but is spoken about, which does not denote, but connotes" in this new context (Jenny, 1976: 267). The patriarchal text undergoes "dialogization" as it becomes relativized, *de*-privileged, aware of competing definitions for the same objective. At the core of the intertextual, lies the feminist poet's rebellion against the language of patriarchy which is undialogized, and absolute (Cf. Bakhtin, 1973:411 passim; Mukarovsky, 1977).

Intertextuality, as a formal strategic component in poetic discourse, allows the poet to make her own text converge with other types of textual productions in order to generate a multiplicity of meanings made cohesive by a specific ideology opposed to patriarchy. Such poetic strategies are aimed at activating the reader's memory: their design produces cultural and historical oppositions between the patriarchal monopoly of discourse and the consequences this monopoly has brought in the production of meanings. Those oppositions create textual *polemics* as *recurrent elements* in poetic discourse by women. The reader's memory is activated and oriented towards the untold, to the unexplored side of women's position in culture. What is revealed, since the 1950's, is a gradually conscious stand against "amnesia", against forgetting, because the word *should* not forget where it has been. This is part of their commitment to find the roots of a female-identified culture, roots that need to be remebered.

The tension between the poet and the alien text may be resolved either by exclusion or inclusion, by the expression - in poetic terms - of an attitude reflected in the utterance of the new message: on the modes in which the alien text is appropriated.

The practice of intertextual strategies in feminist poems begins gradually, subversely to be cultivated and discovered by North-American poets in the 1970's; that is, the alien word starts to take the shape of patriarchal text as the writers gain consciousness in the twentieth century emergence of feminism, about a decade after the period which can be considered the breakthrough in North-American women's poetry, between around 1955 and 1965 (Carruthers, 1979; Ostriker, 1982; McKluskie, 1983; Díaz-Diocaretz, 1983a;1983b). From then on it has continued to be imitated and developed further. Among the precursors in feminist poetic discourse is Adrienne Rich, without whose work feminist writing - at least in English - would have taken perhaps another decade to evolve up to where it is now.

II.2. THE INTERTEXTUAL FACTOR IN THE POETRY OF ADRIENNE RICH

A chronological reading of Adrienne Rich's poetry tracing the intertextual crossings will reveal significant changes in the structuring of the poems, and semantically, will made manifest the trajectory of her dialogue with culture, the continuities and the discontinuities of her multivoiced word, elements which shape an important area of her poetic praxis. The reader is led to follow this procedure in the presentation of direct or oblique textual strategies, and to go beyond the threshold of sources or influences, that is, in accordance with demands of a greater coherence. If the discovery of sources were the main point, then we, as readers, would be left in total mystery as to where some texts come from. But that is not the case with Adrienne Rich's poetry, as she grows more in control of her material. Yet this only refers to the explicit presence of texts. In her first three books, and I would like to emphasize that this covers her poems up to the writing of the title-poem "Snapshots of a Daughter-in-Law", there are no indicators signaling explicit intertextual bonds, a fact which clearly suggests that the poet was not aware of the textual possibilities in the use of the alien text. In the years that follow the writing of the above mentioned poem, Rich indicates the sources for most of the texts she employs.

As a reader of her own poetry, Rich has consistently commented that the process of reading and of writing are interwoven; in re-visioning and re-reading her poem "Snapshots" more than a decade after its composition, she places this text in an epoch in which she dutifully followed cultural and literary models: "It strikes me now as too literary, too dependent on allusion; I hadn't found the courage yet to do without authorities, or, even to use the pronoun 'I' - the woman in the poem is always 'she'" (Rich, 1979b:45). The courage lies elsewhere in the poem, implicitly present in those authorities she could not do without. The inclusion of other texts in "Snapshots", a poem written between 1958-1960, initiates her in what I consider her feminist discourse, extended in that first phase, up to the very last line in her volume <u>Poems, Selected and New</u> (1975), a line which I shall discuss further on in this essay. With her next book, The Dream of a Common Language (Rich, 1978), I place her third phase, of female oriented and female identified poetic discourse.

But let us try to elucidate first what underlies the poet's words when twenty years after writing "Snapshots" she calls this text "the first feminist poem she ever wrote". Here Rich's concept and act of re-vision from a feminist perpective needs to be recalled:

> A radical critique of literature, feminist in its impulse, would take the work first of all as a clue to how we live, how we have been living, how we have been led to imagine ourselves, how our language has trapped as well as liberated us; and how we can begin to see - and therefore live - afresh.
> (1979b:35)

As we suggested in more detail in the previous essay, in 1971 Rich proposes the guidelines of a project for feminist writing and critism, and provides the *definition* of the "act of looking back". Yet the *practice* of this re-vision has already began in her poetry a decade before defining it.

About Rich's first books, A Change of World (1951), The Diamond Cutters (1955), the praise was mainly to her debt to the masters. For W.H. Auden and Randall Jarrell, Rich's echoes of other poets reflected her fitting position as a dutiful poet who was conscious of craft, and who followed and accepted the influence of - among others - T.S. Eliot, Wallace Stevens, Robert Frost, Dylan Thomas, Auden himself, Tennyson, and John Donne. Those masters were what Auden called in his preface to Rich's book, the "family tree" of her poems (Auden, 1975:126). The comments by other critics were, on the whole, similar to Jarrell's view of The Diamond Cutters, in which he signaled relationships between - for instance - Rich's "The Perennial Answer" with "the typical neurotic- violent Frost - with one touch of Robert Lowell -" (Jarrell, 1975:128). There is general consensus among critics and the poet herself that the diction, the prosodic figures, the tone between 'objective' and 'confessional' rendering of experience, and some of the images that serve the poet as motivation, as 'impulse' originate in her readings of those formative years (Gelpi, 1975:132; Rich, 1979b:39-40). In her first two books, and her third, we find images recurrent in English poetry, such as Milton's Satan in "Lucifer in the Train" (Rich 1975:18), or Eliot's "The Waste Land" in "Living in Sin" (Rich, 1975:18-19), and others. All in all, in those formative years, the texts that appear in an indirect, implicit relationship in her poems before "Snapshots" are essentially texts which support the poet's verbal message, which provide a source of inspiration for new meaning, yet a meaning that contributes to an expansion of the poet's *received ideas and images* without further criticism. Meaning is ideologically grounded in agreement between the poet and the world. Thus, the poet follows the persuasive force of the patriarchal word, having "to take the world as it was given" (Rich, 1975:15).

At least four types of shifters are used by Rich to direct the reader's attention to the alien text:

a) Through notes to a number of poems providing the source.
b) Through direct quotations of texts which are often in italics in the poem, as a text-within-the text, thereby indicating the presence of the alien word.
c) By reference to titles, authors, anthroponimic elements.
d) By the use of epigraphs.

Yet these are only a few indicators. More important to describe feminist poetic discourse is Rich's introduction into her text of a partial reversal of a quotation through the change of a single but significant word in order to create implicit internal polemic with the alien text.

The poem "Snapshots" is crucial for the understanding of Rich's interplay of intertextuality, since it already contains the strategies the poet would be using in the future. In that poem, the speaker contemplates with detachment a woman who is defined in a man's world, as daughter-in-law, as wife, as daughter, and mother at the same time; however, this detachment is one in which the speaker's omniscience reveals a poetic tension. We see the transition Rich was undergoing at that time, which anticipates the dialogic development of her work in the next fifteen years. Each section in this poem signals the presence of at least one alien text. Section 2 reads:

> Banging the coffee-pot into the sink
> she hears the angels chiding, and looks out
> past the raked gardens to the sloppy sky.
> Only a week since They said: *Have no patience.*
>
> The next time it was: *Be insatiable.*
> Then: *Save yourself; others you cannot save.*
> Sometimes she's let the tapstream scald her arm,
> a Match burn to her thumbnail,
>
> or held her hand above the kettle's snout
> right in the woolly steam. They are probably angels,
> since nothing hurts her anymore, except
> each morning's grit blowing into her eyes.

The image of the angels chiding is a polygenetic text (a text diachronically related to more than one text): the dialogue of the angel of reality, of the necessary angel of earth in Wallace Stevens's poem "Angels Surrounded by Paysans", (Stevens, 1972:354) is alluded to, angels who are the woman's inner voices, who try to move her to rebel and stop her external inert life, to fight this routine that hurts her. But this inner battle is also linked with Virginia Woolf's image of a "phantom" that haunted her:

> And the phantom was a woman, and when I came to
> know her better I called her after the heroine of
> a famous poem, "The Angel in the House".
> It was she who bothered me and wasted my time and
> so tormented me that at last I killed her.
>   (1942:58)

Inner phantoms, the inner angels also haunt the daughter-in-law. Rich perfoms a congenial reading with Woolf's, creating a context of polemic against yet another earlier text, the one mentioned by Woolf, C.K.D. Patmore's "The Angel in The House" (1862), a long work designated to represent the apotheosis of love in marriage, the progress of deep, pure love amid the incidents of a commonplace life.

The next section of interest of our discussion, is number three:

> A thinking woman sleeps with monsters.
> The beak that grips her, she becomes. And Nature,
> that sprung-lidded, still commodious
> steamer-trunk of *tempora* and *mores*
> gets stuffed with it all:
> the mildewed orange-flowers,
> the female pills, the terrible breasts
> of Boadicea beneath flat foxes' heads and orchids.

Cicero's voice in "Pro Rege Deiotaro" (II.31) appears here, echoed in the "O Tempora! O Mores!" (Gelpi, 1975:13, n.4) to illustrate Nature contextualized now in the daughter-in-law's experience, as full of debasement, and immorality; yet, in the fourth line the polemic begins overtly with Rich's images strictly related to women, making of Cicero's perspective a thought cast in doubt in this ironic twist.
Furthermore, Rich employs an anthroponimic device which is polygenetic through the naming of Boadicea. In addition to being an actual British Queen, Boadicea is a mythical figure, and a text from a well known story. She is a queen remembered for her revolt against the Romans. Interestingly enough, Boadicea's action was the topic of several plays in the nineteenth century, and the central subject of two poems, one by William Cowper (XVIII century poet), the other Alfred Lord Tennyson (XIX century).

William Cowper's ode (1782) was written as a prophesy about the destruction of Rome. Tennyson's "Boadicea", published in 1864, was inspired by an engraving by Thomas Stothard. We should also remember that Boadicea is mentioned by Tacitus: while the Roman governor was destroying the Druids' groves in Anglesey, the Iceni rebelled after Boadicea was 'flogged', her daughters raped, and the land plundered. In Tennyson's poem the breasts of the mother are "chopped". Rich's Boadicea has "terrible breasts", a metonymy for the slaughtering of the women, and of Boadicea's own killing of the women to achieve victory through human sacrifice; as a warrior, she fought tyranny, but was conquered. Now, in Rich's poem, Boadicea is shown as a merely static image surrounded by flowers connoting early twentieth-century ornamentation.

In addition to this type of diachronic relation of a word or phrase in a contemporary context (a method practised by T.S. Eliot in "The Waste Land") in "Snapshots" we find a technique that is characteristic of Adrienne Rich and which was subsequently incorporated in feminist poetry and feminist discourse in general in English. It consists of the use of lexical-semantic repetitions of phrases that come from literary texts or which are part of rhetorical and literary discourse, yet with a very significant change in the gender explicit in the subtext:

> Two handsome women, gripped in argument
> each proud, acute, subtle, I hear scream
> across the cut glass and majolica
> like Furies cornered from their prey:
> The argument *ad feminam* all the old knives
> that have rusted in my back, I drive in yours,
> *ma semblable, ma soeur!*

Feminist discourse, a discourse *ad feminam*, contextualizes the arguments formerly *ad hominem* and from there the woman speaks

> *ma semblable, ma soeur!*

In this last phrase, we hear the obvious omission of a <u>part</u> from Baudelaire's last line in his poem "Au lecteur", with which he begins <u>Les Fleurs du Mal</u>: "Hypocrite lecteur--mon semblable--mon frère!". However, since we cannot forget Adrienne Rich's own tradition, we are also led to hear T.S. Eliot's closing line in Section I of "The Waste Land" consisting of the inclusion not of a portion but of the complete line from Baudelaire's poem.

This is one way in which traditional meanings are reversed as they have been handed down to a supposedly universal world. Rich's critique of what history and literature say about women is carried out through allusions; in "Snapshots", to the time of the Greeks, the Romans, to fifteenth and sixteenth century texts (pastoral poetry and the concept of women therein). Also in this poem, the eighteenth century erudites Diderot and Johnson are quoted in order to have their words and deeds situated within the polemic against patriarchy constructed by the poet; the nineteenth century statements are evoked in a like manner. All these texts are combined, juxtaposed to show that "Time is male" (Rich, 1975:50), and to expose in her re-vision, why women were unsuccessful in becoming part of a culture which has kept them in a marginal or passive role.

The polemic treatment of texts from the past, in different languages (Latin, French, Spanish, German) is given cohesiveness by the speaker's argument poetically developed through contrasts, irony, and re-readings which reveal a search for dialogue with women, and a search for the true and full image of women in culture. After the writing of "Snapshots", the alien texts continue to be present either supporting Rich's vision as she gradually builds her own model of the world, or building paradigmatic oppositions. Other types of texts become predominant within this framework in the books Necessities of Life (1966), Leaflets (1969), The Will to Change (1971), and Diving into the Wreck (1973). By way of example, several ideographic statements from non-linguistic systems appear in a consistent way: it is, clearly, an intersemiotic transposition of images from films, photography, and painting. Equally important are the poetic devices presenting the 'popular culture' contemporary to the poet, and those images which have an intertextual relation with social texts, that is, extra-literary elements as symbols of patriarchal images of women and of society.

In the last text from Poems, Selected and New (1975), titled "From an Old House in America", dated 1974, the last line contains a non-explicit, and enciphered alien text in which, again, the poet made a small but nonetheless significant change (emphasis mine) (Rich, 1975:245):

        Isolation, the dream
        of the frontier woman

>   leveling her rifle along
>   the homestead fence
>
>   still snares our pride
>   ---a suicidal leaf
>
>   laid under the burning-glass
>   in the sun's eye
>
>   <u>Any woman's death diminishes me</u>

The last line is in direct polemic with John Donne's "Meditation XVII: <u>Nunc Lento Sonitu Dicunt, Morieris</u>":

>   Any man's death diminishes me, because
>   I am involved in mankind, and therefore
>   never send to know for whom the bell tolls;
>   It tolls for thee.
>   (Donne, 1959:108)

Rich's poetic reminiscence projected in the above quoted lines goes beyond the argument "man's death versus woman's death" because it challenges the very meaning of "mankind", therefore, of what the word "universal" actually means to men and to women.

Rich's verse marks the significant change and the future direction of her work from her next book <u>The Dream of a Common Language</u>. Her constant questioning of man, of patriarchy, language, socio-cultural constraints, man's freedom and power, finds a polarizing image in John Donne's text mentioned above, which continues with the following:

>   ... and she buries a man, that action concerns me:
>   all mankind is of one author, and is one volume;
>   when one man dies, one chapter is not torn out
>   of the book, but translated into a better language.

The polemic "any woman's death diminishes me" is the main subject of her next two books, where she explores not just the lives of women who do not appear in the book of mankind, but also the relationships and bonds which have existed among women, unspoken, unnamed, "outside the law" (Rich, 1978:31). In <u>The Dream of a Common Language</u>, in order to carry out the re-vision of the world, Rich first demythologyzes patriarchy by continuing the polemic against man's culture and remythologyzes it by giving a female-oriented poetic model of the world. Poem IV of the sequence "Twenty-One Love Poems" illustrates yet another feature:

>.... I open the mail,
> drinking delicious coffee, delicious music,
> my body still both light and heavy with you. The mail
> lets fall a Xerox of something written by a man
> aged 27, a hostage, tortured in prison:
> *My genitals have been the object of such sadistic display*
> *they keep me constantly awake with the pain ...*
> *Do whatever you can to survive.*
> *You know, that men love wars ...*
> And my incurable anger, my unmendable wounds
> break open further with tears, I am crying helplessly,
> and they still control the world, and you are not in my arms.

In <u>The Dream</u>, man is no longer a central part yet he is still a major antagonist. Man's violence continues both outside, as the political flier suggests, and inside through the man in the elevator. In the closure the poet introduces a polygenetic phrase which adds a negative shade of meaning to the semantic fields of "man" and "violence": "... I am crying helplessly,/and they still control the world, and you are not in my arms".

In this section of the twenty-two part interior monologue to a woman, the line just quoted draws attention to the world of patriarchy: the referent of "they" is "men" (on deixis in this context see Díaz-Diocaretz, 1983a, 1983b). The borrowing of the rhythmical components: "and they still control the world ..." grounds the text on the poetic tradition, making her argument deeper. We are led to T.S. Eliot's "The Waste Land":

> Above the antique mantel was displayed
> As though a window gave upon the sylvan scene
> The change of Philomel, by the barbarous king
> So rudely forced; yet there the nightingale
> Filled all the desert with inviolable voice
> And still she cried, and still the world pursues,
> "Jug Jug" to dirty ears.
> (Eliot, 1969:64)

"I am crying helplessly,/and they still control the world, and you are not in my arms.", "And still she cried, and still the world pursues" show how the verbal art comes alive in the dialogical transferral, from one context to another, one poet to another. Furthermore, through Eliot's images brought in by his context of the sylvan scene and the change of Philomela, we are led to evoke Milton's Paradise Lost (IV, 140) and Ovid's Metamorphosis (VI, "Philomela"), respectively. It is with this dialogical interaction of rhythmic figures, and with these imagistic clusters that Rich makes the poem end in a closure which is polysemic yet directed to one central image: Like the barbarous king, like Teru's transgression in the sisters' world - raping Philomela and condemning Procne to silence forever by cutting off her tongue, depriving her thus of *the word* - man continues to cause splits, separating, still in the same way. The twentieth century speaker cries helplessly because she lives in this world she sees as destitute of tenderness, ruled by men who love wars, torture, death.

These two lines I have presented for discussion are one of the few implicit intertextual relations in The Dream which mark the presence of the patriarchal text. As I have suggested earlier, it is in The Dream and in A Wild Patience Has Taken Me This Far that the woman's world takes shape not only semantically, but in the intertextual currents and undercurrents as well. In the two books just mentioned, if we trace the poet's relation to her alien texts, we find that it is not just the possibility to "imagine a world of women only", "a world where men are absent", (Rich, 1978:61), but it is a discourse oriented towards the building up of a *discourse of women* only, where women are no longer *dismembered* but *re-membered* (see Rich, 1978:75).

The intertextual relations in both The Dream and A Wild Patience consists of poetic networks of messages written by women, in which, for example, "old words like integrity" are now used with a feminist meaning, and defined within a feminist context in the "Notes" (Rich, 1981: 61-61). The poem "Culture and Anarchy" - even though it is a title borrowed from Mathew Arnold - directs the reading not to Arnold's text but presents a dialogue of interwoven images and alternating voices of nineteenth century women, counterpointed by the voice of the speaker, a XXth century woman in North-America. Some of the sources used are: the diaries of Susan B. Anthony, Elizabeth Barret-Browning's letter to Anna Brownell Jameson, the speech "On Solitude of Self" by Elizabeth Cady Stanton, and a letter from the latter to Susan B. Anthony. In other poems Rich makes use of passages, phrases, expressions, images from feminist articles, from studies, pamphlets and many others (see Rich, 1981:60-61). Even the social texts from the external world are now those operating within (and referring to) the semantic fields related to "woman" (e.g. "For Julia in Nebraska"). The attempt to construct a discourse of women only, is what characterizes *female oriented* and *female identified discourse*.

Following the development of Adrienne Rich's poetry in a reading that uncovers the poet's relation to the alien text, we can refer to three phases in her poetic discourse -"the graph of a process still going on"-:

1. What I have called, using it only as a working concept, *non-feminist discourse:* 1951 to about 1959. Text which contribute to an expansion of tradition and of the poet's received ideas and images, without a polarizing force, or a clearly identified antagonist, within the patriarchal world. In general, there is a congenial dialogue with the voices of her contemporaries and those who precede her.

2. From about 1958 to about 1975: polemic dialogue employing the texts from patriarchy, as well as a polemic critique of the received ideas.
   Representative of this textual attitude towards the alien text are the lines: "Did you think I was talking about my life?/I was trying to drive a tradition up against the wall" (Rich, 1975: 122). This is a major factor of *feminist discourse*.

3. From about 1974 to 1981: female-identified, female-oriented discourse, in the exploration of woman's world and the woman-to-wo-

man relationship.

Congenial dialogue with texts by women is predominant, as the patriarchal text is still part of and source for antagonistic forces (e.g. "man" is no longer a major presence).

Given this theoretical construct, if we take into consideration not the chronology of Rich's poetic development but the intertextual features outlined from her poetic material, we may find it useful as a programmatic framework, with the working definitions as a mode of articulation of a larger project: to formulate if there are poetic strategies which are specifically practiced by women, and to find the modes of differentiation within the category of *discourse by women* from 1950 to the present. In other words, to prove an intertextual fact in a group of texts as a whole. If we apply this model we shall find substantial differences within the spectrum of "feminism" in the poetry of, for example, the authors I study in another article currently in progress: Anne Sexton, Denise Levertov, Diane Wakoski, Sylvia Plath, Susan Griffin, Judy Grahn, Susan Sherman, June Jordan, Audre Lorde, Olga Broumas, Ntzake Shange, and Margaret Randall. Adrienne Rich herself can be studied under this construct to trace her discourse in the future. Her most recent book, Sources (Rich, 1983) presents us with a poetic voice that is predominantly feminist, since father and husband are important addressees and *major explicit absences* as well.

Whether the alien texts are included or excluded, we cannot deny that writing poetry that is essentially feminist in orientation means being part of the struggle for the images that will express a single consciousness, by means of the word which "can never free itself from the dominion of the contexts of which it has been part" (Bakhtin, 1973: 167). Such is the dialectics between the feminist poet and the alien text.

III. "'NO ONE'S FATED OR DOOMED TO LOVE ANYONE':
    A READING OF 'TWENTY-ONE LOVE POEMS'"

III.1. "THE MEANING OF OUR LOVE"

Since <u>A Change of World</u>, the institutionalized man-woman bond was, for about two decades, the emotional and social *locus* for the speaker's experience; this locus had a wide range. As Adrienne Rich was then making excursions into new territories, she exhibited no open criticism, but was cautious, or was not quite aware of it. Yet, the reader can perceive some irritation underlying earlier poems, such as "Aunt Jennifer's Tigers", and in "An Unsaid Word", (1951), a text we quote in full:

> She wo has power to call her man
> From that estranged intensity
> Where his mind forages alone,
> Yet keeps her peace and leaves him free,
> And then his thoughts to her return
> Stands where he left her, still his own,
> Knows this the hardest thing to learn.
> (Rich, 1975:6)

The title could not be more appropriate. The poet's lexicon presents the oppositions of estrangement/freedom, silence/dialogue. Written as a single sentence carefully balanced in subordinated clauses arranged in iambic cadence, this poem initiates the woman's voice containing hidden tones of inminent awareness of difficulties and constraints; it inaugurates the route which will be followed, the field which would be ploughed.

Rhythm, and the indirect treatment of situations - whether subjective or objective - provided sound points of departure. Some two decades later, by about 1974, the speaker has seen with more precision that explicit rendering. With the force of truth and interpretative power, in "From An Old House in America", the speaker reaches the knowledge and clarity of vision to discover the roots of failure, having lost a sense of location in the realm defined as a "savagely fathered and unmothered world". The woman who stood "Where he left her, still his own" and for whom "this was the hardest thing to learn" speaks now impervious to impositions from without:

>   If I dream of you these days
>   I know my dreams are mine and not of you
>
>   Yet something hangs between us
>   older and stranger than ourselves
>
>   like translucent curtain, a sheet of water
>   a dusty window
>
>   the irreducible, incomplete connection
>   between the dead and the living
>
>   or between man and woman in this
>   savagely fathered and unmothered world
>   (Rich, 1975:237)

Here the speaker is an American woman, embittered by the pain of distance and estrangement. Rich is almost the only woman poet of that time to protest against dissociations created by a male-dominated world. The poet does not confine herself to referring to the external world. The speaker is a careful observer, and has found the place for connections, the place of splits in a *locus* familiar within herself. She becomes conscious - and makes her readers conscious - of the limits and possibilities of her power both within and outside the established man-woman relationship. From an initial acceptance of the discourse of power, Rich moves on and rebells against it. It is in the lonely journey to self-knowledge that she discerns a sense of *arrival* at the meridian of a starting point on the one hand, and the awareness of *departure* from Europe, her ancestry, as an exile from the man-woman relationship on the other hand; the only dream now is "isolation". Such is the central theme of "From An Old House in America", a poem which, like "Snapshots of a Daughter-in-Law" (1958-1960) sets off a crucial movement in the trajectory of Rich's poetic discourse.

Significantly, "From An Old House in America" is the last poem in Rich's work up to the present in which man is "the other" or the "you" as addressee. The volume of poetry that follows, Twenty-One Love Poems, was first issued in a limited edition of 1000 books (1976), and later included as the central section of The Dream of a Common Language. Moving from a feminist to a lesbian/feminist perspective - since man seems to offer and want nothing but frustrations, dominance, destruction - the poet's and the speaker's desire for fulfillment changes direction. The presence of man from there on is scarce in the new texts. History, society, tradition, and other manifestations of patriarchy become forces existing mainly in the background.

Not surprisingly, some male critics failed to recognize the significance of Rich's transformed voice as a lesbian poet, contending, for example, that although she had adopted "an anti-male, frankly sexist" posture, "she also implies that the hope has not been entirely lost of a time when these old words and the vision embodied in them, the 'dream of a common language' may still come true" (Carruth, 1978:84). This reviewer pretends to ignore the fact that the love poems in the central sequence are written by a woman and have as addressee, also a woman. "The hope" then, exists but it has been re-territorialized in the dominion of women. If patriarchy has put the seal of silence on women's words, now Rich provided for that silence the seal of possibilities for this newly discovered women's world to be named and to be allowed existence openly. Such is the context of the "Twenty-One Love Poems" in which love is conceived as a *process* that happens between two people, a relationship defined by Rich in her essay "Woman and Honour: Some Notes of Lying" as:

> An honourable human relationship--that is, one in which two people have the right to use the word "love"-- is a process, delicate, violent, often terrifying to both persons involved, a process of refining the truths they can tell each other.
> (Rich, 1977a:188)

Out of the profound commitment to live under a "new ethics" and a "new morality" as a woman, Rich, once again re-visions her own words: Love must be contextualized in a new light. Conscious of her readers, and moved by her need to be precise or closer to truth, Rich affirms in a parenthetical note, that when she uses the words "personal relationship" in that essay, she means a relationship between two women (1977a:186); both "Women and Honour" and the "Twenty-One Love Poems" were written in about the same period.

In the sequence of love poems Rich offers the reader the possibility of apprehending her meditations conveyed in an intimate, almost confessional tone. Introspection unifies the perspective of the speaker who moves from point to point in a poetic monologue where the procession of visions, the emotional momentum flow in a calm lyric stream "into the unfinished/the unbegun/the possible" (1978:5).
Poet and *persona* commingle in the sequence: "Close between grief and anger, a space opens/Where I am Adrienne, alone. And growing colder" (1978:XVIII, 34).[9] The space from where her voice rises is the *personal*, however, no solipsism is claimed. The underlying marginalization of women in diverse societal and cultural functions is one of Rich's important continuities in her critique of the contemporary world *via* her poetry and prose. Unsatisfied, and aware of the world which is unfavourable and fragmenting to women, Rich shares the goal with feminists of instilling the uncreated conscience of selfhood and identity for women. Modernist and contemporary feminists have begun to uncover a society that is split by the masculine/feminine paradigmatic polarities, and to reject the traditional stereotypes passively accepted in the past. This is not sheer rebellion; it is a serious attempt to understand and communicate women's real identity, to salvage what remains in spite of numerous cultural strains. Yet this is only one phase, a primary stage which nourished the political impulse of much of the first and second wave of feminism in the twentieth century in the United States. A descendant of that struggle can be seen in the direction lesbian/feminist writing is undertaking, a natural offspring of inner forces guiding the speaker in the course of images in order to move forward into new forms of revelation of female complexity (1977:228).

Thus Rich no longer reacts against the patriarchal world as she used to do in the past, but acts towards a new present in which her own act of writing will point to the world of relationships among and between women. If man is mentioned in the sequence, he appears only incidentally, as a distant presence, as an outsider to this womanly, female world. In the background there is the insistence that the speaker is no longer living - internally - in man's world.

III.2. LIMITLESS DESIRE, LIMITLESS LANGUAGE

The thematic and formal principles of the lyrical and meditative sequence of love poems are structured by the vision of love as a *process*, as a journey that originates in the mental landscapes, the domestic interiors in the lives of two women, and in the external settings internalized and transformed by the women's wisdom and power. There is a dialectic of togetherness and separateness. The journey of discovery leads the speaker as *poet, lover* and *traveller*, inwards into the mind. The first and the last poems provide a key in this respect:

> Wherever in this city, screens flicker
> with pornography, with science-fiction vampires,
> victimized hirelings bending to the lash,
> we also have to walk ... if simply as we walk
> through the rainsoaked garbage, the tabloid cruelties
> of our own neighborhoods.
> We need to grasp our lives inseparable
> from those rancid dreams, that blurt of metal those
> disgraces,
> (I, 25)

> An this is not Stonehenge
> simply nor any place but the mind
> casting back to where her solitude,
> shared, could be chosen without loneliness,
> not easily nor without pains to stake out
> the circle, the heavy shadows, the great light.
> I choose to be a figure in that light,
> half-blotted by darkness, something moving
> across that space, the color of stone,
> greeting the moon, yet more than a stone:
> a woman. I choose to walk here. And to draw this circle.
> (XXI, 36)

The poet's re-collection and re-discovery of what has happened take her from the city where she begins the journey with her lover, towards her inner space, where she eventually chooses to "walk" alone, returning to her own self, confirming her presentment in poem XX: "and soon I shall know I was talking to my own soul" (p. 35).

In the twenty-two sections, we can discern the making of a manifold dream. On the one hand, it is presented as a hope for understanding and being understood; as an expression of all the desires and wishes that arise from the intimacy between two women; and as a determination to conquer the mutual, common fears, so that the failures in the past help them discover a viable future. This is particularly relevant for the poems in which the *present* and *future* tenses predominate.

On the other hand, the dream is a re-collection of the lover's images in the act of writing, which brings the speaker awareness of their love and its meaning in the world – both inner and outer – a meaning that comes as an "arquitecture", a "pure invention" (XIII), a "work heroic in its ordinariness" (XIX), and at the same time a "miracle" (XVIII), in their love. The dream is also the act of being re-membered; the vision of the difficulties and risks involved in trying to reach, to grasp together the sacred and the hidden connections of their love. Poems VIII, XIV, and XV especially, written predominantly in the *past* tense, convey a reflection of a past being re-experienced, made real in the mind by way of re-membrance.

The dream-quality of the sequence is reinforced by the interplay of past, present and future. As an example, poem XII begins in the present:

>   Sleeping, turning in turn like planets
>   rotating in their midnight meadow:
>   a touch is enough to let us know
>   we're not alone in the universe, even in sleep

then a textual reference to time appears:

>   and the past echoing through our bloodstream
>   is freighted with different language, different meanings--

Finally, in the same poem, the speaker's mind moves into timelessness through the vision of a yet unwritten chronicle, thereby incorporating their love as a recorded experience (emphasis mine):

>   though in any chronicle of the world we share
>   *it could* be written with new meaning

>   *we were* two lovers of one gender,
>   *we were* two women of one generation.
>   (XII, 30-31)

With the reiteration of "we were", the poem leaves the lovers in a past which has not happened in reality yet, but which becomes articulated in the imagination.

Another example worth considering is "The Floating Poem, Unnumbered". Here the poet creates and re-creates their lovemaking in an interplay of present and future. This mutual search and touching is transformed into a timeless encounter, not because it belongs out of time but because if fuses time in a hypothetical present and in its continuation - in the mind - of the "here-ness" and "now-ness" of their love:

>   Whatever happens with us, your body
>   will haunt mine--
>
>   ... --whatever happens, this is.
>   (p. 32)

This memory of their lovemaking becomes then a present that is made permanent and transcendent. The distinction between the predominant use of either present or past fulfills its function in the structure of the sequence, but in each poem there is not a clear distinction since the three main levels of time sway in a triadic motion, fused in the form of a dream. Nothing is spared in this creative act of the imagination because even the past has its inviolate place, it is the past recreated through language, a past which is "familiarly risen in the midst of the present, with that rather unreal complexion of things which a kind of illusion makes us see a few steps ahead": [10] because the past in the "Twenty-One Love Poems" is not simply contemporary; in the imagination it is the space where one can connect oneself even with ancient times:

>   I want to travel with you to every sacred mountain
>   smoking within like the sibyl stooped over her tripod,
>   (XI, 30)

If we are to find the real time of the sequence, we can situate it in the poem's "corporeality", in their *presentness* and *presence*.[11] The moment of poeticizing, that is, the act of imaging through which the poems spatialize themselves, is the poet's remembrance, the re-captured memory in a fresh vision set as a constant movement.

The present rises as a solitary but enlightening awareness of what <u>was</u> and *is* beautiful, of what has caused pain. The experience, lived anew, remains as another state of consciousness and as a "heroic" illusion— a knowledge that the lovers are together and at the same time that each is subsumed in her own "circle".

The private experience of a dream brings revelations, consciousness of dangers; the mind wanders freely gathering the unconscious, and when awaken, it reconsiders those images and it transforms them into thoughts; in Rich this is not idle thinking, or day-dream. "Time", is still "male"; there is no place for free-play or fantasy; in the *substratum* we read the urgent need to understand the true nature of events not as they are given to the poet but as they are conceived by her. It is also in this context that the sequence gains full meaning. The verbs "wish", "want", "desire", "dream", "wonder", "feel", "know", and the like, recur in the poems.

In poem I, the wish to survive, to rescue and be rescued by the other from the terror and corruption of the external, everyday world of the unatractive city with its garbage, its "tabloid cruelties", is what establishes the necessity to make their relationship exist, to "name it", to connect it with the world. This allows the lovers to delineate the boundaries of what draws them together, and to define the borders of their safe *territory*. Rich's attitude of "moving forward" implies that both lovers can exist and enter a new world where they can be themselves, because "no one has imagined" them. In the stifling atmosphere of the city, the necessity "to live like trees", (I) in the open, in love, grows in spite of the "sulfuric air". It is their common desire to settle for life, with a love that does not deny sexuality, but which makes it part of its foundation; with their roots clasped tight under the city, the earthy ground. They want to survive, away from those "rancid dreams", to plunge into the world of the feminine unconscious, the unrepressed forces within themselves. In poem II, Rich's dream of her lover being a *poem* offers an example of the correlation she establishes between the unconscious, reality, and poetry: "<u>I dreamed you were a poem</u>, I say, *a poem* I wanted to show someone ..." (p. 25). In "Women and Honour" Rich states:

> The unconscious wants truth, as the body does.
> The complexity and fecundity of dreams come
> from the complexity and fecundity of the un-
> conscious struggling to fulfill that desire.
> The complexity and fecundity of poetry come
> from the same struggle.
> (1977a:188)

Truth is the force directing individual experience; "when a woman tells the truth she is creating the possibility for more truth around her". Poem II postulates the need to assume an act of determination as a strong way of achieving this: "I want to know even our limits". Once limits become visible the infinite possibilities of love can also be discovered. Mortality is the first impending limit, and instead of being nihilistic about it, the poet clings to the capacity to live thoroughly *because* of this inminent danger. The poem's closure confirms this: "Somehow, each of us will help the other live,/and somewhere, each of us must help the other die" (III:26).

Throughout the "Twenty-One Love Poems", Rich reveals how the closeness between two women is attained in spite of distance. The key to this is the conscious, shared use of their power. Having the willingness to "help" (III) is a commitment that is possible through a collective faith. Man's world, Rich suggests in poem V, is violent, and women must contribute not to make of their world a similar one. In poem VI, the poet introduces the image of a woman's hands as the potential for female violence, but above all, for tenderness. They have essentially life-giving function. Moreover, these hands have a tremendous potential for power and danger if necessary, yet they can be controlled:

> with such restraint, with such a grasp
> of the range and limits of violence,
> that violence ever after would be obsolete.
>
> (p. 28)

Thus women are able to fight a public, hostile world and turn to a private, tender, bonding existence; if pain - both physical and spiritual - is caused or can be caused by the violence of the outside world, it is to be endured without self-pity, for a woman can heal her wounds, can fight her suffering rather than nurture it; the task is easier if done with the loved one rather than without her:

> ...The woman who cherished
> her suffering is dead. I am her descendant.
> I love the scar-tissue she handed on to me,
> but I want to go on from here with you
> fighting the temptation to make a career of pain.
>
> (VIII, 29)

Love as a process of refining the truths two people can tell each other also requires speaking out, naming what has remained unnamed up to now. This change implies the shaping of a new world, with new principles, with a new language, because "women's love for women has been represented almost entirely through silence and lies" (1978). In the first poem of the sequence, Rich affirms: "No one has imagined us", referring to the complete dismissal of close women's relationships with women in the past. Everything must be re-discovered because

> Whatever's lost there is needed by both of us--
> a watch of old gold, a water-blurred fever chart,
> a key. ... Even the silt and pebbles of the bottom
> deserve their glint of recognition.
>
> (IX, 29)

But the act of cognition cannot be done in isolation, for the "absolute and primary attention declared at the other" is a common, shared purpose:

>   ...show me what I can do
>   for you, who have often made the unnameable
>   nameable for others, even for me.

The possibilities for connections exist in language:

>   I want to reach for your hand as we scale the path,
>   to feel your arteries glowing in my clasp,
>   never failing to note the small, jewel-like flower
>   unfamiliar to us, nameless till we rename her.
>   (XI, 30)

Not only the inner aspects of life must be named, but the external ones that are, at times, more powerful as well, because by internalizing them - giving them their own meanings - they can make the "drive to connect" possible:

>   that detail outside ourselves that brings us together,
>   was here before us, knew we would come, and sees beyond us.
>   (XI, 30)

The fact that no one has reached the space of their encounter before, that the *locus* of their love is an unexplored world, is to be seen as a challenge, a possibility to give themselves up to the journey:

>   We're chasing the raven and the wren
>   through gorges unexplored since dawn
>   whatever we do together is pure invention
>   the maps they gave us were out of date
>   by years ...
>   (XIII, 31)

This exploration has a physical *locus*, which is not an end in itself, but which brings them to greater proximity in lovemaking. "The Floating Poem, Unnumbered", presents the sexual experience as a liberating, mutually gratifying dialogue between and through their bodies, naming each other with tenderness, reaching a fulfillment which is both ancient and new:

>   the innocence and wisdom of the place
>   my tongue has found there-- ...
>
> your strong tongue and slender fingers
> reaching where I had been waiting years for you
> in my rose wet-cave--
>
>   (p. 32)

These are the possibilties beyond the limits, Rich suggests, if we are willing to find truth, the 'fibers of actual life as we live it', the light we are starved for. The cleansing "desperation of our search" is not free from suffering, but one must "touch the wound beyond the wound" (1978:63). This implies having to find the roots of failure, by exploring the private pain that haunts, and the obstacles that are not just personal, but collective. This is one of Rich's profound beliefs - growing deeper every year, that women share more than they are aware of, for the difference between herself and her lover - in the "Twenty-One Love Poems" - is at the same time the difference with other women:

>   But we have different voices, even in sleep,
>   and our bodies, so alike, are yet so different
>   and the past echoing through our bloodstreams
>   is freighted with different language, different meanings--
>   (XII, 30)

Yet what is *common* lies in the infinity these differences can create. Furthermore, exploring the reason for separation, or distance, brings about a complex set of circumstances, and forces the lovers to face the obstacles and dangers women must come across, dangers they did not choose; a woman *in* a man's world, but not *of* it, the poet knows that the dangers, among others, are political: "I am crying helplessly,/and they still control the world, and you are not in my arms" (IV:27). It still needs to be recalled that literature has given women a negative self-image: "Goethe's dread of the Mothers, ..." (V). Regardless of the kinship felt with each other, there is a split that is older than themselves, for they "have different voices, even in sleep,/and (their) bodies, so alike, are yet so different" (XII). They are inevitably separated, isolated like the woman "drowning in secrets", with "fear wound round her throat/and choking her like hair" (XX). Even poetry, the act of naming with images, seems to be insufficient for a complete connection:

> or, when away from you I try to create you in words,
> am I simply using you, like a river or a war?
> And how I have used rivers, how I have used wars
> to escape writing of the worst thing of all--
>
> (VII, 28)

"Language cannot do everything", Rich writes in "Cartographies of Silence" (1978:19), but lovers can try, even in spite of being like "dream-ghosts of two worlds/walking their ghost-towns" (XII), walking, living in tenderness, for without it, "we are in hell" (X).

The forces separating the lovers are not only "within" them, but also "against" them (XVII); the will to understand the love relationship which can survive those forces leaves the poet with a double awareness that she has been "talking to her own soul" (XX) and, at the same time, that she has a vision of truth reflected in her lover's soul that is like her own. She has found, in her journey, that true love begins in the self and to the self returns. And in this process she has crossed the threshold of her own truth to be shared in the honorable relationship of

> "... two women, eye to eye
> measuring each other's spirit, each other's
> limitless desire,
>
> a whole new poetry beginning here".

NOTES

1. Rich's work and critical essays have appeared in Ms., American Poetry Review, The New York Review of Books, The New York Times Book Review, The Washington Post Book World, Chicago Review, The Nation, College English, Poetry. Rich has lectured in many prestigious universities and also at the MLA.

2. Many of Rich's poems have appeared in Crysalis, Amazon Quarterly, Field, Heresies, The Little Magazine, Moving Out, New Boston Review, 13th Moon, Conditions, Iowa Review, Maenad, Sunbury, Massachusetts Review, indeed a wide variety of literary magazines. Her work has been translated into Japanese, Italian, Dutch, French, and Spanish.
Caedmon House has produced two records of her readings; also important are the records "Adrienne Rich Reading at Stanford" (1973) with an introduction by Barbara Ch. Gelpi, and jacket notes by Albert Gelpi, issued by The Stanford Program for Recordings in Sound, and "A Sign/I was not Alone" (1977) with Honor Moore, Audre Lorde, and Joan Larkin, produced by Out & Out Books. Between 1980-1983 Rich edited and published the lesbian-feminist journal Sinister Wisdom with Michelle Cliff.

3. Rich (1979c:78) defines the patriarchal world or patriarchy as follows: "I mean to imply not simply the tracing of descent through the father, which anthropologists seem to agree is a relatively late phenomenon, but any kind of group organization in which males hold dominant power and determine what part females shall and shall not play, and in which capabilities assigned to women are relegated generally to the mystical and aesthetic and excluded from the practical and political realms".

4. When we oppose *verbal art* as such and art as a communicative function we are following Bakhtin (1973:261, 294). According to him, lyrical poetry appears to be authentically a work of *verbal*

art, due to its choice and combination of words, subordinated to the aesthetic project. Within the communicative-function area, words direct our attention to thematic aspects quite abstracted from *pure-y verbal* considerations. Rich has given her discourse a "social life".

5. This has been particularly evident after Rich's writing of <u>The Dream of a Common Language</u> (1978) and her essays on lesbian feminism. Refusing to define her literary work as private craft, Rich has insisted on asserting what we have called the social life of her discourse in her decision to write *about, to* and *for* women. If readers interpret Rich's poetry in other ways, the poet feels there has been a betrayal of her work: "Two friends of mine, both artists, wrote me about reading the <u>Twenty-One Love Poems</u> with their male lovers, assuring me how 'universal' the poems were. I found myself angered, and when I asked myself why, I realized that it was anger at having my work essentially assimilated and stripped of its meaning, 'integrated' into heterosexual romance. That kind of 'acceptance' of the book seems to me a refusal of its deepest implications" (Bulkin, 1977b:58). In her latest essay on "Compulsory Heterosexuality and Lesbian Existence" Rich (1980) develops further the idea of the "lesbian *continuum*" for women's existence.

6. On this subject see Díaz-Diocaretz (1980; 1982; 1984a; 1984b).

7. Eco (1976:75) starts from a discussion of a general system for the content-form in structural semantics organizing culture into sub-systems, fields, axes (see Guiraud, 1955; Ullmann, 1963; Lyons, 1963; Greimas, 1966; Todorov, 1966). According to Eco, "semantic fields give shape to the units of a given culture and establish portions of the world vision belonging to that culture" (Eco, 1976:76); Eco (p. 289) further defines a semantic system or sub-system as "one possible way of giving form to the world. As such is constitutes a partial *interpretation* of the world and can theoretically be revised every time new messages which semantic-

ally restructure the code introduce new positional values". Therefore, a Global Semantic System consists of the totality of semantic systems in a given civilization. Eco (1979:68) illustrates the use of this concept as follows: "Finnegan's Wake, at this point, presents itself as an excellent model of a Global Semantic System (since it posits itself, quite explicitly, as the Ersatz of the historical universe of language) and confronts us with a methodological exigency of the sort found in a study of general semantics proposing to illuminate the ways in which language can generate metaphors".

8. In "Compulsory Heterosexuality" Rich (1980:650) writes: "As the term 'lesbian' has been held to limiting, clinical associations in its patriarchal definition, female friendship and comradeship have been set apart from the erotic, thus limiting the erotic itself. But as we deepen and broaden the range of what we define as lesbian existence, as we delineate a lesbian continuum, we begin to dicover the erotic in female terms: as that which is unconfirmed to any single part of the body or solely to the body itself, as an energy not only diffuse but ... omnipresent ... and in the sharing of work".

9. The Dream of a Common Language, New York: Norton, 1978. Subsequent references to "Twenty-One Love Poems" will be to this edition.
The Roman number specifies the poem, the Arabic number, the corresponding page.

10. Marcel Proust, On Reading, trans. J. Auret and W. Burford (Norwich: Flechter & Son, 1971), p. 67.

11. For a theoretical analysis of the "presentness" and "presence" of a poem, see Krieger (1976:207-245).

REFERENCES

I - ADRIENNE RICH

Rich, Adrienne (Cecile). 1951. A Change of World.
　　　　　　New Haven: Yale University Press.

──────────. 1955. The Diamond Cutters and Other Poems.
　　　　　　New York: Harper and Row.

──────────. 1963. Snapshots of a Daughter-in-Law.
　　　　　　New York: Harper and Row.

──────────. 1964. "Poetry and Experience: Statement at a Poetry Reading". In Gelpi 1975:89.

──────────. 1966. Necessities of Life: Poems 1962-1965.
　　　　　　New York: Norton.

──────────. 1967. Selected Poems.
　　　　　　London: Chatto & Windus.

──────────. 1969. Leaflets: Poems 1965-1968.
　　　　　　New York: Norton.

──────────. 1971. The Will to Change: Poems 1968-1970.
　　　　　　New York: Norton.

──────────. 1973. Diving into the Wreck: Poems 1971-1972.
　　　　　　New York: Norton.

──────────. 1975. Poems: Selected and New, 1950-1974.
　　　　　　New York: Norton.

──────────. 1976a. Of Woman Born: Motherhood as Experience and Institution. New York: Norton.

──────────. 1976b. Twenty-One Love Poems.
　　　　　　California: Effie's Press.

──────────. 1976c. "Foreword". In J. Bankier et al., eds.
The Other Voice: Twentieth Century Women's Poetry in Translation. New York: Norton.

──────────. 1977a. Women and Honour: Some Notes on Lying.
　　　　　　Pittsburgh: Motheroot Press. Rpt. Rich 1979:185-194.

──────────. 1977b. The Meaning of Our Love for Women Is What We Have Constantly to Expand. New York: Out & Out Books. Rpt. Rich 1979:185-194.

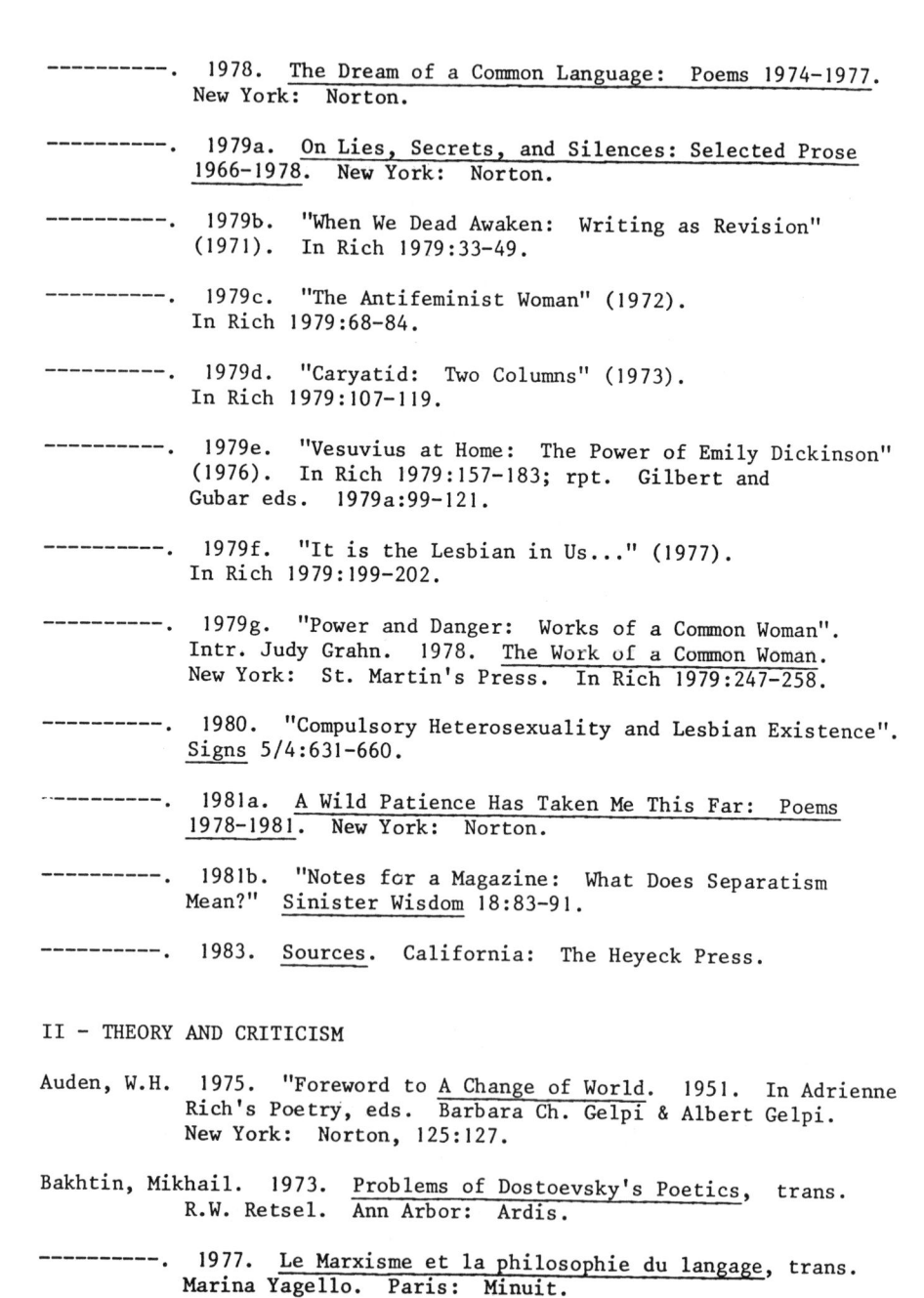

----------. 1978. The Dream of a Common Language: Poems 1974-1977. New York: Norton.

----------. 1979a. On Lies, Secrets, and Silences: Selected Prose 1966-1978. New York: Norton.

----------. 1979b. "When We Dead Awaken: Writing as Revision" (1971). In Rich 1979:33-49.

----------. 1979c. "The Antifeminist Woman" (1972). In Rich 1979:68-84.

----------. 1979d. "Caryatid: Two Columns" (1973). In Rich 1979:107-119.

----------. 1979e. "Vesuvius at Home: The Power of Emily Dickinson" (1976). In Rich 1979:157-183; rpt. Gilbert and Gubar eds. 1979a:99-121.

----------. 1979f. "It is the Lesbian in Us..." (1977). In Rich 1979:199-202.

----------. 1979g. "Power and Danger: Works of a Common Woman". Intr. Judy Grahn. 1978. The Work of a Common Woman. New York: St. Martin's Press. In Rich 1979:247-258.

----------. 1980. "Compulsory Heterosexuality and Lesbian Existence". Signs 5/4:631-660.

----------. 1981a. A Wild Patience Has Taken Me This Far: Poems 1978-1981. New York: Norton.

----------. 1981b. "Notes for a Magazine: What Does Separatism Mean?" Sinister Wisdom 18:83-91.

----------. 1983. Sources. California: The Heyeck Press.

II - THEORY AND CRITICISM

Auden, W.H. 1975. "Foreword to A Change of World. 1951. In Adrienne Rich's Poetry, eds. Barbara Ch. Gelpi & Albert Gelpi. New York: Norton, 125:127.

Bakhtin, Mikhail. 1973. Problems of Dostoevsky's Poetics, trans. R.W. Retsel. Ann Arbor: Ardis.

----------. 1977. Le Marxisme et la philosophie du langage, trans. Marina Yagello. Paris: Minuit.

----------. 1981. The Dialogic Imagination: Four Essays, ed. Michael Holquist, trans. C. Emerson & Holquist. Austin: University of Texas Press.

Barthes, Roland. 1979. "From Work to Text", in Textual Strategies: Perspectives in Post-Structuralist Criticism, ed. José V. Harari. Ithaca: Cornell University Press, 73:81.

Black, Maria and Coward, Rosalind. 1981. "Linguistic, Social and Sexual Relations: a Review of Dale Spender's Man made Language", Screen Education, 39.

Bulkin, Elly. 1977a. "An Interview with Adrienne Rich". Part I, Conditions: One I/1:50-65.

----------. 1977b. "An Interview with Adrienne Rich". Part II. Conditions: Two I/2:53-71.

Boyers, R. 1975. "On Adrienne Rich: Intelligence and Will". In Gelpi, ed. 148-160.

Brown, Howard J. 1976. "In Secret, In Public". New York Times Review, October 21:39.

Carruth, Hayden. 1978. "Excellence in Poetry". Harper's, September, pp. 81-87.

Carruthers, Mary. 1979. "Imagining Women: Notes Towards a Feminist Poetic". The Massachusetts Review 20, 2:281-307.

Clemons, Walter. 1975. "Adrienne Rich: A Retrospective". New York Times Book Review, April 27:5.

Corti, Maria. 1975. Principi della Comunicazione Letteraria. Milan: Bompiani.

Dällenbach, Lucien. 1976. "Intertexte et autotexte", Poétique 27: 282-296.

Daly, Mary. 1976. Gyn/Ecology. The Metaethics of Radical Feminism. New York: Beacon Press.

Díaz-Diocaretz, Myriam. 1980. "Passion by June Jordan", Thirteenth Moon V, 1&2:147-155.

----------. 1982. "Black Sister: Poetry by Black-American Women, 1746-1980", Thirteenth Moon VI, 1&2:137-143.

----------. 1983a. Reading and Writing in the Act of Translation: The Poetry of Adrienne Rich. Ph.D. diss. State University of New York at Stony Brook. Ann Arbor: University Microfilms International.

----------. 1983b. "Homosocial Arrangements: From Concept to Discourse", in Among Men, Among Women: Sociological and Historical Recognition of Homosocial Arrangements, ed. Mattias Duyves et al. Amsterdam: Sociologisch Instituut, University of Amsterdam: 441-449.

----------. 1983c. "Een brug slaan tussen vertalen en vrouwenstudies", trans. Ria Lemaire, in Kongresbundel: Winteruniversiteit Vrouwenstudies 1983: 52-57.

----------. 1984a. "Black North-American Voices: The Poetry of G. Brooks, L. Clifton, M. Evans, N. Giovanni, A. Walker and J. Jordan" limited edition, Lesbisch Archief, Leeuwarden, The Netherlands.

----------. 1984b. "Black North-American Women's Poetry and the Semiotics of Culture", Paper for the conference "Women, Feminist Identity, and Society in the 1980's", First Session of the Utrecht Summer School of Critical Semiotics, Rijksuniversiteit Utrecht, The Netherlands.

Donne, John. 1959. Devotions Upon Emergent Occasions. Ann Arbor: University of Michigan.

Duplessis, Rachel Blau. 1979. "The Critique of Consciousness and Myth in Levertov, Rich, and Rukeyser", (1975). In Gilbert and Gubar, eds.: 280-300.

Eco, Umberto. 1976. A Theory of Semiotics. Bloomington: Indiana University Press.

----------. 1979. The Role of the Reader: Explorations in the Semiotics of Texts. Bloomington: Indiana University Press.

Eliot, T.S. 1969. The Complete Poems and Plays. London: Faber & Faber.

Elshtain, Jean B. 1982. "Feminist Discourse and Its Discontent: Language, Power, Meaning". Signs: Journal of Women in Culture and Society, 7, 3:603-618.

Foucault, Michel. 1979. "What is an Author?". In Harari ed. 141-160.

Geckeler, Horst. 1976. Semántica estructural y teoría del campo semántico. trad. M. Martínez Hernández. Madrid: Gredos.

Gelpi, Albert. 1973. "Adrienne Rich: The Poetics of Change". In Rich: 1975, 130-148.

---------- and Barbara C. Gelpi, eds. 1975. Adrienne Rich's Poetry.
New York: Norton.

Genette, Gérard. 1979. Introduction à l'architexte. Paris: Seuil.

Gilbert, Sandra, Susan Gubar, eds. 1979b. The Madwoman in the Attick:
The Woman Writer and the Nineteenth Century Literary Imagination. New Haven: Yale University Press.

Grahn, Judy. 1978. The Work of a Common Woman.
New York: St. Martin's Press.

Greimas, A.J. 1966. Sémantique structurale, Recherche de méthode.
Paris: Larousse.

Griffin, Susan. 1978. Woman and Nature: The Roaring Inside Her.
New York: Harper Colophon.

Guiraud, Pierre. 1955. La Sémantique. Paris: PUF.

Iser, Wolfgang. 1978. The Act of Reading: A Theory of Aesthetic
Response. Baltimore: The Johns Hopkins University Press
(German ed. 1976).

Harari, Josué V. ed. 1979. Textual Strategies: Perspectives in Post-
Structuralist Criticism. Ithaca: Cornell University Press.

Jarrell, Randall. 1956. "Review of The Diamond Cutters and Other
Poems". In Adrienne Rich's Poetry: 127-129.

Jenny, Laurent. 1976. "La stratégie de la forme", Poétique 27: 258-281.

Jong, Erica. 1975. "Visionary Anger (1973): In Gelpi, ed.: 171-174.

Krieger, Murray. 1976. Poetic Presence and Illusion: Essays in Criti-
cal History and Theory. Baltimore: The Johns Hopkins
University Press.

Kristeva, Julia. 1968. "Poésie et négativité", L'Homme 2 (VIII) avril-
juin: 36-63.

----------. 1969. Semiotikè: Recherches pour une sémanalyse.
Paris: Seuil.

----------. 1974. La révolution du langage poétique. Paris: Seuil.

----------. 1980. Desire in Language, ed. Leon S. Roudiez, trans.
Thomas Gora et al. New York: Columbia University Press.

Lotman, Jury. 1976. Analysis of the Poetic Text, trans. D. Barton
Johnson. Ann Arbor: Ardis.

Lyons, John. 1963. Structural Semantics: An Analysis of Part of the Vocabulary of Plato. Oxford: Blackwell.

Marks, Elaine. 1979. "Lesbian Intertextuality", in Homosexualities and French Literature, eds. George Stambolian & Marks. Ithaca, New York: Cornell University Press: 353-377.

Martin, Wendy. 1975. "From Patriarchy to the Female Principle". In Gelpi, ed.: 175-188.

McKluskie, Kate. 1983. "Women's Language and Literature: A Problem in Women's Studies", Feminist Review 14 (June): 51-61.

Millett, Kate. 1970. Sexual Politics. Garden City, New York: Doubleday & Co.

Mukarovsky, Jan. 1977. The Word and the Verbal Art: Selected Essays, trans. and ed. John Burbank & Peter Steiner. New Haven: Yale University Press.

Ostriker, Alicia. 1982. "The Thieves of Language: Women Poets and Revisionist Mythmaking", Signs: A Journal of Women in Culture and Society 8, 1: 68-90.

Proust, Marcel. 1971. On Reading, ed. trans. Jean Autret & William Burford. Norwich: Fletcher & Son.

Ricardou, Jean. 1971. Pour une théorie du nouveau roman. Paris: Seuil.

Schwarz, Judith. 1979. "Questionnaire on Issues in Lesbian History". Frontiers IV, 3: 1-12.

Rusinko, Elaine. 1979. "Intertextuality: The Soviet Approach to Subtext", Dispositio 11/12: 213-235.

Showalter, Elaine. 1979. "Towards a Feminist Poetics", in Women Writing and Writing about Women, ed. Mary Jacobus. New York: Barnes and Noble: 22-41.

Stevens, Wallace. 1972. The Palm at the End of the Mind: Selected Poems and a Play, ed. Holly Stevens. New York: Vintage.

Spender, Dale. 1980. Man Made Language. London: Routledge and Kegan Paul.

Taranovsky, Kiril. 1976. Essays on Mandelstam. Cambridge: Harvard University Press.

Todorov, Tzvetan. 1966. "Perspectives Sémiologiques". Communications II: 28-39.

Tynianov, Jury. 1965. Théorie de la littérature. Paris: Seuil.

Ullman, Stephen. 1962. Semantics: An Introduction to the Science of Meaning. Oxford: Blackwell.

Vendler, Helen. 1973. "Ghostlier Demarcations, Keener Sounds". In Gelpi, ed.: 160-171.

----------. 1981. "All Too Real", The New York Review of Books, December 19: 33-36.

Woolf, Virgina. 1942. The Common Reader: First Series. New York: Harcourt.

PS
3535
.I233
Z63